The Federal Republic,
Europe,
and the World

Norwegian Foreign Policy Studies No. 31

Martin Sæter

The Federal Republic, Europe, and the World

Perspectives on West German Foreign Policy

Universitetsforlaget

Oslo - Bergen - Tromsø

327.43
S127f

© Universitetsforlaget 1980
ISBN 82-00-05315-6
Translated from Norwegian by Susan Høivik
Cover: Oddvar Wold
Printed in Norway by
Tangen-Trykk, Drammen

Distribution offices:

NORWAY
Universitetsforlaget
P. O. Box 2977, Tøyen
Oslo 6

UNITED KINGDOM
Global Book Resources Ltd.
109 Great Russell Street
London WC1B 3Nd

UNITED STATES and CANADA
Columbia University Press
136 South Broadway
Irvington-on-Hudson
New York 10533

80-8063

Acknowledgement

This study was originally written for the *Research Institute of National Defence* (FOA) in Stockholm as one of several discussion papers prepared for the comprehensive FOA project about the foreign policies of the Western countries. I am grateful to FOA for letting me publish my paper as a book. I want to thank the leader of the project, Dr. Gunnar Jervas, for his able and inspiring organizing of the seminar discussions, from which I profited very much. Among the other staff members of FOA, Professor Nils ·Andrén deserves my special thanks for his kind assistance. I should also like to stress how much I valued the criticism and advice given me by Mr. Åke Sparring, the Director of the Swedish Institute of International Affairs, who had task of being the chief commentator on my manuscript.

Lest it should be misunderstood, the aim of the study was not to arrive at some general consensus on the views presented, but rather to be provoking in a constructive way, trying to direct attention to aspects of West German foreign policy that are of crucial importance for developments in the whole of Europe. For the opinions expressed I am, of course, alone responsible.

November, 1979.
M. S.

Contents

I. Introductory remarks

The Federal Republic of Germany is today an essential actor within the international system. By this is meant that its location and policies are pivotal in determining the character of the international system, both structurally and with respect to interaction. And by 'structure' we are referring to the international division of power, organization, and various more permanent forms and patterns of interaction.

It was primarily in connection with the partition of Germany following World War II that the bi-polar bloc structure became crystallized – a structure that throughout the post-war period has been decisive for the European, indeed the global, security-policy situation. With its geo-strategic position in the heart of Europe, the Federal Republic of Germany – the strongest power in Western Europe militarily and economically, and the USA's major supporting actor – will under any circumstances necessarily occupy a central position in any and all questions concerning fundamental changes in the structure of the international system. This vital role is further strengthened by the fact that West Germany today is also the leading nation with respect to Western European integration.

Finally, as yet another indication of Bonn's potential influence, mention should be made of the special status of the FRG as concerns international law; and the FRG's close connections, through treaties and practical politics, with other nations and groups of nations.

It is a striking feature of the position and political development of the FRG that those very restraints that were originally intended as means to exert one-sided control/influence on the part of other states vis-à-vis the policies of West Germany, have gradually and increasingly changed character: they have in fact become strings that Bonn can pull to exert influence on its former 'guardians' and on the international scene generally. An explanation of this may be found in the FRG's increased military, economic, and political power, as well as in the fact that the FRG has, by means of its 'Ostpolitik' and its policy of detente, freed itself from the onus of World War II. But it is important to bear in mind the distinctive aspects connected with this development, aspects often denoted in the literature by the keywords *penetration, interdependence,* and *integration.*

A nation's political system is 'penetrated' to the degree that non-members of the system may participate directly and authoritatively in the allocation of social goods, or in mobilization of support for various political goals. From its very beginnings, the Federal Republic of Germany has been perhaps the most penetrated national system in Europe – at any rate, of the major states. However, the effect of penetration need not always be identical with one-sided dependency. The answer to this question will depend on the ability of the state or system concerned to utilize the penetration channels the other way round, to reverse the flow so to speak. Penetration and one-sided dependency may be transmuted into interpenetration and mutual dependency or interdependence. On the basis of such considerations, it is clearly correct to speak of the Federal Republic as being 'an influential, powerful, and penetrated system'.[1]

That developments should have taken this turn is also connected to the question of integration. Previously one-sided control measures were gradually replaced by integration arrangements with a non-discriminatory basis. Through integration into NATO and the European Community, the Federal Republic gained its sovereignty at the same time as the integration and indispensability of West German contributions made it natural for previous one-sided dependency to turn into a mutual situation of interdependence. That the 'German question' is still formally held open through clauses in the FRG Constitution and in the maintenance of Four Power responsibility for 'all Germany' represents perhaps an equally great limitation on the freedom of action of the allies as on that of West Germany today.

In recent years the relevance and importance for West German policy of the interdependence question have increased in two ways. First, the concept of 'Ostpolitik' is built on the tenet that the age of the 'policy of strength' is over, and that only through meaningful cooperation and rapprochement on the basis of mutual interest can there be any hope of bringing the two Germanies closer. Second, international politics in general have in the 1970's undergone a remarkable change in the direction of linkages, both explicit and implicit, between more traditional forms of alliance and security policy, on the one hand, and other sectors of a state's policy – primarily the economic sector – on the other hand. The 1973 oil crisis and global negotations on a New International Economic Order may serve as illustrations here. On various levels – inter-German, regional European, global – the Federal Republic is vitally interested in forms of 'complex interdependence' which can help to provide security with a stronger non-military basis, and which can at the same time be suitable instruments for converting the FRG's great economic potential into foreign policy influence.

Extending the concept of security to include non-military aspects, whether with respect to East-West policy or the question of a New International Economic Order; the inability of existing alliances to serve as coordinating fora; uncertainty concerning the goals of detente policy and of the European Community: these are all issues that raise fundamental questions as to the organization of international politics and thereby the structures of today's international system as well. That such issues have mutual and reciprocal connections – not least as shown by developments within the European Community – means that a choice of solutions and approaches in specific areas may well appear as 'strategic' choices of fundamental importance in a more general sense.

For instance, should approaches to detente and the German question be based on the idea of a permanent status quo in Europe – with maintenance of the two Germanies and of the current bloc structure – or should the goal be discontinuation of the partition of Germany and de-escalation of superpower hegemony in Europe? Do recent US efforts to achieve improved Western coordination – under US leadership – in the fields of foreign policy, security policy, and economic policy within NATO and the OECD, mean that East-West bloc politics, hitherto based on military-strategic priorities, are to be transformed into a more inclusive and comprehensive system of global bloc politics? If this were the case, would such a line be compatible with the goals of detente? And how do possibilities for development in these areas relate to today's EC perspectives? What are the necessary preconditions for continuing the present intergovernmental kind of Community leadership in the attempts at political and economic union? To what extent could such an EC model be compatible with set guidelines in the German question, with the goals of detente, with the above-mentioned US coordination line within NATO and the OECD? These are but a few of the questions that arise.

Because of its considerable weight in terms of military-strategic, economic, and political potential, there seems to be every reason to expect that the FRG will continue to play an important, in part decisive, role with respect to the choice of mutual 'solutions' in various vital contexts, as well as in the concrete formulation and implementation of multilateral plans.

From what has been said above it should be clear that the area of concern in this study is both extensive and complicated. With respect to the major aim of our study – to clarify alternative developmental lines for West German foreign and security policy – the difficult question arises: which analytical approach is most adequate? Obviously, our main interest concentrates on those aspects of West German policy which are of major future relevance to other European countries in the context of foreign policy and security – and this in turn brings in East-West relations in general, superpower relations, the alliances and other multilateral frameworks, the position of neutral countries, North-South relations, etc. There would thus seem to be good reasons for a *structural analysis* on the international system level. In this way it might be easiest to shed light on the central position of the FRG and its importance in these contexts. *Historically,* however, the foreign and security policies of the Federal Republic have been decisively linked with developments in the German question, so that continuity – or lack of such – is best studied in relation to these developments.

If we chose as our point of departure a structural analysis of the international system, this would involve first trying to determine the more permanent aspects of Bonn's international environment. Then, on the basis of this analysis, we would proceed to the current West German situation and try to isolate which alternative perspectives might be realistic/probable, given the existing international framework and existing West German goals and priorities.

On the other hand, if we chose to start with the German question as focal point, our analysis would be more directed towards clarifying current goals, priorities, and possible alternatives to this policy.

10

Then we would confront this policy with the policies of other states and with international structural determinants, hoping in this way to shed light on possibilities of realizing such aims, probable choices of strategies, national and international consequences, etc.

These two approaches differ from each other mainly in the order in which the various analytical operations are performed. In both cases it would be necessary to take into consideration factors and conditions on both the national and the international level. However, choice of explanatory factors, and thereby also the character of the explanations, may vary according to which approach was chosen – and this may in turn influence our bases for prediction. Basically, methodological prediction problems will be the same, whether on the national or the international level. For our purposes it seems most fruitful to start out from the national FRG level, seeking to identify main aspects of the existing situation – including historical trends and interrelationships with the international environment – and then to project conceivable lines of development into the future, always working on the basis of certain ideas of what seem to be relevant or interesting possibilities, and what do not. Thereafter, these findings will be tested on two 'higher' levels of analysis, that of the European Community and the Atlantic one, to see what might be regarded as more or less probable future lines of development.

The unique historical development of the Federal Republic would seem to indicate policies concerning the German question as a natural point of departure for analysis of the period up to the Ostpolitik of the early 1970s. Because of the central importance of the German question in East-West relations and in matters of alliance and integration policy, and because of the special legal and political status of the Federal Republic as a 'penetrated' national system, any analysis of the development of the German question must necessarily also be concerned with the policies of the superpowers and other actors as well – thereby touching on the general area of international politics. This is further emphasized by the fact that, after the conclusion of the bilateral treaties with the Eastern Countries, the Ostpolitik stressed a 'multilateralization' of West German policy in the German question within the frameworks of the EC and the CSCE – and this still forms the basis of Bonn's policy.

The year 1973 marks a watershed in various ways. For one thing, by 1973 it had proved possible, by means of Ostpolitik and detente, to remove the major conflict-creating issues in connection with the German question. Further, the above-mentioned 'multilateralization' came into view; and East-West relations gradually became overshadowed by global North-South problems in the wake of the 'oil crisis'. Thus 1973 marks a turning point, after which it becomes natural to place analytical emphasis on West German foreign and security policies on the 'systems level'. With respect to future perspectives for these policy areas, developments within the European Community will be particularly relevant.

As long as the Federal Republic continues to use the EC as a framework for its own policy in the German question and in other areas of foreign-policy relevance, various alternative solutions as to the inner development of the Community itself, its role in Western cooperation, in East-West relations and in global politics as a whole will necessarily also act as determining factors in the options open to West German politics. Further expansion of political cooperation within the EC, towards an independent political union, will doubtless mean a considerable change in the global power structure. Such cooperation will also open other perspectives for West German foreign and security policy than would be the case were EC cooperation to be limited to individual sectors, or were it to stagnate or be abandoned totally.

On the other hand, the question of which direction the European Community is to take, depends very much on Bonn itself. Furthermore, as earlier mentioned, there exist a close connection and a considerable degree of mutual dependence between the two aspects: the development of the European Community, and developments in such organizations as NATO and the OECD – with regard to East-West and to North-South relations. This in turn touches on existing and potential possibilities of conflict in relations with the United States, possibilities which are not solely limited to NATO and East-West relations but which increasingly involve global issues. There is considerable confusion as to how future EC-USA relations should be organized, and clarification of this problem seems a necessary precondition for defining the role of the Community in other connections as well. There is good reason to see current clashes of interest between the USA and EC countries as a major cause of the slow-down in Ostpolitik dynamics from 1973 onwards.

The earlier-mentioned linkages between various levels and issue-areas make it natural for us to shift attention for the post-1973 period away from a historical-descriptive analysis based on developments in the German question and on Ostpolitik. Instead, we shall concentrate on a more multidimensional 'sytems analysis'.

The aim of such an analysis is first and foremost to create a better foundation for evaluating West German policy in interaction with international surroundings in a future perspective. Here the historical-descriptive portion of our analysis can serve as a point of departure for sorting out which international aspects and which levels are most relevant for our purposes. The first step in our multidimensional analysis will be to clarify the various levels separately, the idea being to sketch relevant, probable, and/or possible developmental perspectives. Next we compare the various levels to see which perspectives are compatible and could be combined in a unified policy, which perspectives are not compatible but perhaps represent alternative models, and finally which perspectives are totally unrealistic and can therefore be eliminated as future developmental possibilities. The concluding step in our analysis will be to discuss the possibilities that still remain open, with the aim of finding out probable action strategies and developmental perspectives for West German foreign policy and security policy.

Naturally such a procedure cannot possibly reveal final answers to all the questions raised. After all, in international politics it is frequently the case that problems are not 'solved' – only suppressed or replaced/overshadowed by other, more important issues. Unexpected chains of events and changes can create new possibilities or eliminate ones that had seemed open. And there will always be obscurities and problems of interpretation. On the other hand, there are historical bases for asserting – at any rate, as far as West German politics is concerned – that major changes do not occur as great leaps, but rather as the result of comprehensive, long-lasting and intense conflicts on both the national and the international level. Bonn's need to define the German question on the basis of internationally recognized contractual agreement, together with the close connection between national West German policy and policy in such multinational fora as the EC, NATO, OECD, CSCE, etc., make it reasonable to count on a considerable degree of continuity in these areas. Even following such dramatic crisis-situations as 1966, when the Erhard government had to yield to the Kiesinger/Brandt coalition, the new line in East-West relations was still largely predictable on the basis of discussions that had taken place publicly between parties and in the press.

What follows immediately is thus the historical-descriptive analysis. We shall have a look at various alternatives and choices with which Bonn has been faced. Our aim is to show why certain of the alternatives were not to be realized – whether by choice or necessity. Here we shall emphasize problem-areas of relevance for future-oriented perspectives. It will also be advantageous for our further analysis if it should prove possible to determine whether certain perspectives that formerly appeared relevant have since been eliminated by the course of historical developments. Inevitably, of course, our historical survey will be brief and summary.

II. The era of bloc dominance: 1949–1969

Fictitious choices

The partition of Germany came about as a result of World War II and succeeding East-West conflicts in Europe. It was a fait accompli before German politicians had a chance to exert any influence on the outcome. The process of partition, which lasted several years, was also a process that fitted each of the two halves into its own part of the two antagonistic alliance systems. There is a close interrelation between partition, alliance membership, and sovereignty. Paradoxical as it may sound, the Federal Republic of Germany became sovereign to the same degree that it let itself be integrated into the Western alliance. And the more integrated it became, the more the cleft of partition deepened.

Decisions as to the occupation of Germany, division into zones, the amalgamation of the Western zones, currency reforms – all these were taken quite independently of German authorities. The reason was that there existed no German authorities competent to negotiate such issues.

However, the founding of the Federal Republic of Germany could not be decided on without German participation. Here leading West German politicians were faced with a choice: not partition or unity, but whether to institutionalize the de facto partition. The alternative to the establishment of a West German state would have been a prolonged regime of occupation; and such a regime would probably not have been able, in the long run, to cope with economic and political difficulties. To let the existing status quo continue indefinitely would have meant risking the rise and growth of radical political tendencies as well. And on one point the Western allies and their German partners did agree: West Germany was not to become Communist. It was on the basis of this fundamental identity of interests that a compromise was finally negotiated.

Just as it may be asserted that West German policy never had a real choice between unity and partition, so there was never a real choice between independence and integration. As mentioned earlier, the actual choice was between integration coupled to the hope of gradually regaining some measure of sovereignty, on the one hand, and a prolonged regime of occupation with all its dangers and disadvantages on the other hand.

Konrad Adenauer – leader of the Christian Democratic Union (CDU) and later Chancellor of the Republic – was probably quite aware of the seriousness of this choice. For him, as for so many other West German politicians, the very character of integration was of decisive importance. In Adenauer's opinion, the proposed West German state could, as a member enjoying equal rights and privileges in a European federation, renounce certain rights of sovereignty. However, he was definitely opposed to any kind of unilateral West German renunciation, reacting sharply to control measures considered necessary by the Western powers, e.g. the international Ruhr Authority.

The agreements between the occupying powers and the new West German state granted to the former party quite considerable rights, especially in military, foreign policy, and constituional questions. The precondition was that these controls were gradually to be lessened, provided this could take place without endangering European security. The Allies made it clear that the sovereignty of the new state would be extended apace with West German assurance that the new government was working for the establishment of a democratic Germany according to the Western pattern.

Adenauer pursued the integration line in the face of intense opposition, especially from the Social Democrats. Towards the Western powers he utilized any and every favourable opportunity to expand the sphere of authority and freedom of action of the Federal government in Bonn. And of decisive importance in this connection was the intensification of the East-West-conflict.

To what extent the Soviet Union would have been willing to accept an independent or neutralized Germany must remain an open question. Moscow's repeated suggestions in this direction in the early 1950s indicate that the Soviets expected more of neutralization than did their Western counterparts. Particularly the Soviet communiqué of 10 March 1952 to the three Western powers created expectations in the Federal Republic, but it was rejected by both the Western powers and the Federal government. This unleashed intense controversy within the Federal Republic as to whether this was not a lost golden chance. In 1952, however, the West German government had no possibility of conducting negotiations with Moscow on its own, since the occupation statutes were still in force. It was not until 1955 that the FRG gained sovereignty in the area of foreign policy, and this in connection with NATO membership – which in turn meant stronger ties with the West. Any solution of the German question without the approval of the Western powers was as unthinkable as a solution without Soviet approval would have been.

Such total dependence on the Western powers in the sphere of foreign policy was the price the FRG had to pay for entrance into the international community. The partition of Germany – and thereby the entire unsolved German question – was a *consequence* of the East-West conflict: and neither the Soviet Union nor the Western powers would yield an inch. In the Western view, there was nothing to be gained from neutralization of Germany, since the West had the greater share of the country within its sphere of influence anyway. For the Soviet Union, however, there was less to lose and more to gain by neutralization, since that would force the West into considerable military withdrawal at the same time as Moscow increased its chances of exerting influence on all of Germany. And it was precisely this that the Western powers wished to avoid. Because of these totally incompatible standpoints on basic principles the sole 'realistic' alternative to German alliance policy – neutrality – was abandoned.

Although Adenauer viewed the West as an ideological unit and saw no contradiction between European and Atlantic cooperation, he clearly meant something more concrete by European 'union' than Western 'unity'. What he had in mind was a true West European Federation, with its own economic policy as well as it own defence and foreign policy. Such a federation would, together with the USA, act to defend Western social and human ideals. In other words, Adenauer was aiming at an integrated Western Europe in close collaboration with the USA. If the Federal Republic of Germany were to be integrated into the Western defence system, this should take place not within NATO but within the proposed European federation, the 'EDC' (European Defence Community). The fiasco of the EDC changed the situation completely. Since rearmament of the FRG had already been decided upon, since such rearmament could – for reasons mentioned above – take place only on the basis of integration, and since there no longer existed any European alternative, the result was that the Federal Republic became integrated into the Atlantic alliance.

As a consequence of its integration into NATO, the West German state was to become militarily more closely and above all more directly tied to the USA than it would have been if the European union had become a reality. The German question became more a Soviet-US question – especially when the Eastern side made the countermove of establishing the Warsaw Treaty Organization, in which East Germany, The German Democratic Republic (GDR), was also included. Just as West Germany became tied to the West through NATO, the GDR became tied to the East through the WTO, and the partition of Germany became further deepened.

Would then the FRG have had any possibility of refusing to join NATO? What exactly was involved in the decision? There seems no doubt that a West German 'no' would have meant prolongation of the occupation regime – which probably would not have served the cause of European integration, or reunification of Germany either. Nor would it have ended the East-West conflict in Europe. Neutralization, as mentioned above, was out of the question. Moreover, refusal would have had negative consequences for relations between the West German government and the Western powers, and Bonn considered the latters' military guarantee an absolute necessity.

Opposed to all this were the advantages inherent in West German membership in NATO. Through NATO, the Federal Republic received the sovereignty due to an indepedent state – albeit with reservations: in questions of foreign policy the Western powers reserved for themselves the right to handle issues concerning 'Germany as a whole'. The forces of occupation were to become 'stationed' armed forces. The West German government was expressly given the right to speak on behalf of all Germany; and in the Paris Treaty of 1954 the Western powers promised to support reunification. They also guaranteed the security of the Federal Republic and of West Berlin.

The insufficiency of bloc politics

It seems unlikely that Adenauer himself believed in any immediate

18

reunification, probably considering this achievable only in connection with political unification of Western Europe. On the basis of his reactions to the unsuccessful European Army, it seems that he was aware of the difference between Atlantic and European integration as regards both European unification and German reunification. All the same, Adenauer believed West European unity to be possible only through the good offices of the United States. He saw the Cold War as an integrating force: faced with the presumed danger from the East, Western Europe would be more or less forced to unify. Adenauer became a convinced 'cold warrior'. In his view, Western Europe was too weak to protect itself against Communism, so it would have to unify under the US protective umbrella. Power and concord within the West were for Adenauer a necessary precondition for successful European integration and German reunification. This formed the background of the so-called 'policy of strength'.

The major dilemma of this policy was that increasing Western unity and strength meant proportionally decreasing chances for Soviet approval of German reunification on Western terms. Strengthening the West meant at the same time strengthening the US engagement in Europe and the leading role of the US there. And the more the US assumed main responsibility for European defence, and the stronger Western defence vis-à-vis the Soviet Union became, the less did Europeans feel any need to push through European integration themselves.

By 1955 the partition of Germany was completed, with the two new states anchored in their respective alliance systems and without the slightest chance to break free from this 'integration'. Their freedom of action in the sphere of foreign policy was proportional to their alliance dedication. Any arrangement concerning the German question seemed possible only on the basis of East-West agreement. During the process of partition, both parts had taken sides on the German question, sides that were to prove incompatible.

The West German stand was that the Federal government, as the sole legitimate German government, had the right to speak on behalf of all Germany. Any reunification would have to take place on the basis of free elections, and the reunited Germany would be allowed freely to determine its foreign policy and alliance policy – the assumption of course being that it would choose to side with the West.

As to the Eastern view, the 1955 Geneva Conference marked the beginnings of Soviet use of the so-called 'two-state doctrine'. Prime Minister Bulganin asserted that in the 10 years that had passed since the close of the war, 'there had been formed two Germanies – the German Democratic Republic and the Federal Republic of Germany – each with its own economic and social structure'. In his speech in East Berlin on 26 July 1955, Khruschev, then Party Secretary, also supported such a two-state theory, and added that settling the German question had now become more difficult, since two German states had arisen. He expressly mentioned the GDR's 'social advances', which could not be sacrificed. It was therefore up to the Germans to find a solution for themselves. Khruschev was in favour of reconciliation between the GDR and the FRG:

> These two German states could, in the interests of the entire German people, create collaboration in all areas of the interior life of Germany, which would without doubt ease the solution of German reunification.[2]

However, as long as these two German states belonged to different alliance systems, Khruschev saw 'no real possibilities' of reunification. The long-range goal of Soviet policy on the German question, then as now, became apparent in a speech by Khruschev in the Supreme Soviet on 29 December 1955:

> If it may truly be assumed that the two German states, currently members of opposing groups, could successfully take part in a common European security system to replace the present two groupings, then the question can be solved in a manner compatible with the interests of the peoples.[3]

With the rearmament of the Federal Republic under NATO auspices, German neutralization was no longer an option for the Soviets. And the realization by both East and West that their standpoints were mutually exclusive and incompatible was to introduce a new phase in the East-West confrontation in Europe, a phase which in practice meant consolidation of the status quo. Since this also meant consolidation of the partition of Germany, the clash between the goals of reunification and Western integration became intensified in West German politics. The incongruence between the Atlantic and the West European framework became more evident. West European union remained a long-term aim, and for this purpose cooperation with France was considered just as fundamental as alliance with the USA.

During negotiations on the Fouchet Plan on political union in the EC there was fairly comprehensive coordination between Paris and Bonn; indeed, of France's partners, West Germany was the one that most strongly supported the Plan. Bilateral consultations between the two countries were intensified after the six-power negotiations had come to an impasse. De Gaulle now advocated a French-German union along the lines of the Fouchet Plan, a union that would serve as a lever for later realization of the Plan itself. The goal remained the same, only the procedure changed.

Underlying France's policy was de Gaulle's desire to organize French-German cooperation, and later six-power cooperation, along confederate lines. De Gaulle further wanted to reorganize Atlantic cooperation towards a more traditional form of alliance; he was also looking for a sort of 'power-sharing' with Moscow, something to remove the divisions between East and West in Europe and make an end of superpower hegemony in both parts of Europe. In order to realize such a programme, de Gaulle needed Adenauer's support. And this was promised him, if he in return would agree to support West Germany on the reunification issue. Here, however, de Gaulle set the precondition that the 'German people' should accept the existing boundaries and instead pursue a policy directed towards entering into a treaty-based, all-European framework for security and cooperation.

On 22 January 1963 the French-German treaty on cooperation was formally signed in Paris. It embraced areas of foreign policy, defence, and culture. In foreign-policy matters of joint interest – and here the existing arrangements and European political cooperation were mentioned, as were East-West relations and problems connected with NATO, the Council of Europe, WEU, and OECD – the signatories were to consult with each other in advance, 'en vue de parvenir, autant que possible, à une position analogue'. As to strategic and tactical issues, the relevant authorities in the two countries were to attempt rapprochement of their doctrines 'en vue d'aboutir à des conceptions communes'. Finally, in cultural matters French-German cooperation was primarily to concentrate on education and youth-exchanges. The agreement provided for meetings between heads of state and government at least twice yearly, and between ministers in the relevant areas at least four times a year.

In both the French-West German cooperation treaty and the Fouchet Plan one finds the same ideas of foreign policy coordination that were later to appear in the Davignon Report and the Tindemans Report. Indeed, these ideas have today become institutionalized in the European Community through the establishment of the conferences of foreign ministers and the European Council, to which we will return below. In the 1960s, however, these ideas were not acceptable to the administration in Washington. On important issues Bonn was torn between Washington and Paris. Relations with Washington became strained because of the West German fear that the superpower dialogue would strengthen the military and political status quo in Europe and in Germany.

Behind the Kennedy Administration's new strategic doctrine of 'flexible response' lay strong motives of arms control. Also in keeping with this line was the increased US interest in a dialogue with Moscow concerning stabilization of the nuclear race. The negotiating forum for these issues was to be, among others, the 18-power CCD in Geneva – where, however, France had refused to participate.

Parallel with attempts to stop an uncontrollable pace of developments in weapons technology, there was also a tendency towards attempts to stabilize political antagonisms. This was natural enough, since the two could scarcely be viewed separately as long as the underlying aim was to limit the risk of war. What was needed for an effective programme of arms and crisis control was, in the US view, a unified military-political leadership of the alliance, particularly with respect to nuclear weapons and East-West relations.

It was in relations with Bonn that the new US attitude first created conflict. US-British negotiating strategies vis-à-vis Moscow were seen, by West German members of the government and other politicians, as expressing a willingness to accept the status quo in Europe in return for greater stability in East-West relations in general. However, such an increase in stability would have to be paid for by political concessions from Bonn on the German question. The limited US reaction to the building of the Berlin Wall in August 1961 came as a psychological shock in West Germany. The thesis that Western strength and cooperation would bring about German unity – and this had always been the official West German justification for alliance membership – was dealt a death-blow. Strengthening an alliance not preoccupied with surmounting the partition of Germany would, in the view of many Germans, be tantamount to sealing the partition.

West Germany's unwillingness to grant concessions that might be interpreted as recognition or strengthening of the status quo was criticized in the US and elsewhere in Western Europe. This in turn strengthened the scepticism and resistance in West Germany with regard to 'detente'. The West German government was faced with a situation where, if it insisted on the original justification for alliance membership on the reunification issue, it now risked political isolation within the alliance.

Against this background, West German-French rapprochement becomes especially important. France had been the only one of the Western allies that categorically refused to negotiate with the Soviet Union on Berlin and Germany as long as Moscow persisted in threats, and as long as the issue at stake was clearly mere stabilization and not elimination of the superpower confrontation in Europe. De Gaulle recognized German unity as a legitimate aim of West German politics, on condition that there be no demand to revise existing borders, and that any any reunification should take place within 'une organisation contractuelle de toute d'Europe'. And as an alternative to 'power politics' in NATO, he presented Bonn with the idea of a strong unified Western Europe able to re-establish the political 'balance' in Europe, to eliminate superpower confrontation and the East-West division, and, given time, to create a framework for German unity.

The more alliance policy was characterized by status quo policy, the more did de Gaulle's alternative appear the sole realistic way to overcome the partition of Germany and of Europe. It must also be borne in mind that the West German government was, on account of its voters, obliged to justify its policies as reunification policies. This, in addition to what was felt as disregard of continental European interests also in the area of security policy, made de Gaulle – on behalf of France – appear as a spokeman for West German national interests, interests which the West Germans themselves were in no position to advance at that time within the alliance.

Rapprochement between West Germany and France – with political union as the express goal – represented a combination of aims which the US could not accept. Officially the US still supported West German demands for reunification, albeit adding that this was a question that could only be regulated after East-West relations in Europe had been 'normalized' – i.e. after the two superpowers had agreed on the major conflict issues in Europe. Seen in isolation, the French policy did not represent a threat to US interests. But a West German policy of reunification coupled to the French independency-line in a formal political union would in reality mean that Washington would lose control both of controversial political issues and of military confrontation questions. This was incompatible with the Kennedy Administration's priority on strategic issues, not least in the field of arms control. US military engagement in a Western Europe that went its own ways would be as unacceptable as US military withdrawal without corresponding Soviet concessions.

When Washington, as late as till the early 1960s, supported the expansion of the European Community in the direction of political union, this was on condition that the status quo should be accepted until such time as it might be possible to find other solutions compatible with US security interests. Of course this meant that the US would take part in formulating any alternative solutions. A political union dominated by France and West Germany would not provide the necessary guarantees here: on the contrary, such a union could be expected to lead to US interests being abandoned in order to obtain possible Soviet concessions to West Germany and France.

The fate of the US proposal to establish a multilateral nuclear force (MLF) in NATO helped, perhaps more than any other single issue, to kill the myth of 'Atlantic' integration being on a par with 'European' integration.

The debate concerning the MLF went on for almost three years without leading to agreement, and in the process managed to uncover conflicts within the alliance rather than strengthen cooperation. To begin with, it was not only France who opposed the plan: other Western European countries proved to be highly reserved and unconvinced. Adenauer, who had originally said yes, later turned sceptical indeed. But after Adenauer was succeeded by Erhard as Chancellor, the West German government supported the plan whole-heartedly, on the assumption that it would grant to West

Germany an effective voice in decision-making on issues concerning the use of nuclear weapons, thereby compensating for what were considered weaknesses of the strategy of 'flexible response'. Great Britain agreed to the plan, but half-heartedly and then mainly because it would ensure American leadership in nuclear strategy and act as a guarantee against Western Europe developing into a 'third power'. This motivation was underlined when the new Labour government presented its alternative proposal of a Atlantic Nuclear Force (ANF).

Among the so-called 'Europeans' too there were many who supported the MLF plan for reasons quite different from those of the US. Whereas Washington viewed the plan as a means to consolidate central leadership of nuclear strategy and to keep NATO together under US leadership, Jean Monnet's influential 'action committee' supported the plan because they saw it as a way to help create a united Europe with its own nuclear force.

The longer negotiations on the project dragged on, the more clearly articulated did the various conflicting interests involved become. Relations between Bonn and Paris suffered, and this made progress in EC questions more difficult. London's support declined as concrete plans were aired for direct influence in nuclear matters on the part of the European allies – that is, mainly from Bonn. And Washington's interest declined as reactions began to show that it would become difficult to combine the US idea of central nuclear control with Bonn's demand for real decision-sharing – and this was a demand which, paradoxically enough, appeared only in the course of, and as a consequence of, MLF negotiations themselves.

The US had never intended to grant the European side a share of the final decision-making power with respect to US or alliance nuclear weapons. As this became clear, the MFL project became more and more vulnerable to 'Gaullist' arguments that the entire plan was but an attempt to strengthen US hegemony over Western Europe. The fact that negotiations gradually turned into a pure US-West German dialogue placed Bonn in danger of becoming politically isolated on the Continent. In the meantime, France's unyielding opposition left no doubt that should the plan be realized, it could shatter the NATO alliance.

The MLF debate had wide-ranging consequences for attitudes towards Atlantic and West European integration. It demonstrated that there had never been a climate for a true Atlantic political union, and furthermore, that there was little chance that the US would in future agree to power-sharing in the decision-making process when the issues at stake were of vital foreign policy or security importance. These two points were irrefutably connected: without political union, a common decision-making process was impossible.

This helped to create a more sobre, pragmatic attitude in Western Europe towards Atlantic cooperation. Especially in West Germany, it became clearer that if the aim was to be political union, it would be necessary to distinguish between the Atlantic and the West European levels. And since an Atlantic federation, a real Atlantic partnership, was now out of the question, the sole possibility lay in Western Europe. This in turn meant that France would have to be included. However, the Federal Republic was far too bound to the US with respect to security policy to be able to work together with France against the will of Washington. Bonn therefore chose to give priority to the EC, trying to develop it towards political communality as far as possible, without having to choose between Washington and Paris in matters of security policy. A process of agonizing reappraisal of the very foundations of West German foreign policy had begun.

For many years, West Germans had been hearing that Bonn's integration policy would solve their national problems. Atlantic defence union, West European economic and political integration, amicable relations with France – all these goals had been presented by leading West German politicians as forming the basis for a coherent policy which would provide the necessary strength to regain national unity.

France's withdrawal from NATO in spring 1966 was for West Germany the final proof that it was totally illusory to speak of European and Atlantic integration as being compatible goals. Without France, European political integration was an impossibility; and without such integration as a goal, the bottom suddenly fell out from under the policy Bonn had so long been pursuing.

This meant that the Atlantic alliance lost much of its *political* importance for West Germany: NATO was no longer a means to West Germany's long-range political goals. And without long-range political goals, no government can hold out against its opposition for long. The West German cabinet crisis of autumn 1966 meant the final defeat of both Bonn's and the Western powers' policy in the 'German question' to date. The crisis had been brewing for many years; in fact it was built into the FRG's situation from the very beginning. Point by point, official West German national policy had run aground because it contained goals which in the final resort proved irreconcilable.

Trying to increase the pace of European integration by strengthening NATO had proved an illusion. By continuing to maintain good relations with the US, the FRG had considerably lessened chances of a coordinated French-German European policy; and such a policy was a precondition for any successful West European political union.

With respect to reunification, it had – as already mentioned – proved illusory to believe that reunification could be achieved by strengthening NATO. Erhard's hope that German participation in a multilateral NATO nuclear force would increase chances of German reunification might sound highly unrealistic, but was most likely a renewed expression of the fact that no West German government could afford to disregard the goal of reunification, still strongly desired by much of the population.

The 'policy of strength' had failed as early as in the 1950s, with the start of superpower status quo policy. All the same, Bonn still hoped to topple the East German regime through economic and political isolation of the GDR. After the construction of the Berlin Wall in 1961, which put an end to East-West work migration, this hope was gradually abandoned as well.

The FRG's demand to act as sole voice for the German people – a demand still supported by the alliance partners – had by now become as unrealistic and illusory as the notion that the GDR could simply be 'incorporated' into the Federal Republic. It was widely realized that reunification could not be brought about as the result of a single operation, but – if at all – only by means of a process, a gradual growing-together of the two disparate social systems. From this it naturally also followed that reunification required close preparatory collaboration between the two German states. East German authorities could not be forced into such collaboration – not even by Moscow, since the basic underlying condition was precisely that Moscow's influence on the GDR would henceforth gradually be reduced in the same way as the US influence in the FRG. The key to

German reunification thus lay not only in Moscow, but also in Pankow.

A strategy aimed at 'isolating' the GDR through a coordinated 'peaceful engagement' in Eastern Europe (minus the GDR) to lessen Eastern interest in the maintenance of the GDR as a state was thus predestined to fail. The thought of a reunited Germany held as little appeal for Germany's Eastern neighbours as for its Western neighbours. On the contrary, for them the GDR represented a guarantee against a too-dominant Germany. And the GDR itself would only be pushed closer into Moscow's arms through such a policy of isolation.

As far as Moscow was concerned, the fact was that the more the other Eastern countries became independent, the more necessary did it become for Moscow to strengthen its hold on the GDR, so as not to lose all control of the situation in Central Europe. It seemed hardly conceivable that Moscow would find attractive such a 'peaceful engagement' as the one the FRG intended – led by Washington and implying increased US and West German economic and political influence not only on the GDR but also on the other Eastern European countries. Detente and 'peaceful engagement' vis-à-vis Eastern Europe, coordinated through the Atlantic alliance and led by the US, could not possibly lead to German reunification: for the simple reason that such reunification was unthinkable within the framework of the existing alliance systems.

The Atlantic alliance, which, according to West German views, was to render possible West European political unity and thereby German reunification, had proved inadequate. The main reason was the difficulty of political collaboration with France; another was the fact that alliance policy was and had to be a policy of status quo, and this in practice excluded any notion of reunification. 'Western integration' had thus lost the major portion of its meaning for West Germany. Events had shown that it was only the Federal Republic that was to be 'integrated'; while states like Great Britain and France could act as privileged nuclear powers, and the great protector – the US – both in its European policy and through its engagement in areas geographically outside the Atlantic alliance, was primarily interested in attending to its own superpower interests. It was the US that dictated alliance strategy, and this frequently against the views of Bonn. Costly weapons systems suddenly became 'obsolete' and had to be replaced by new ones, perhaps even more costly. The Germans often felt that the decisive factor was not so much the defence of Western Europe, as furtherance of the interests of US industry and commerce. Both the US and Great Britain threatened to reduce their forces in Western Germany unless the costs of maintaining them were fully reimbursed by Bonn.

In addition, there was the general feeling that no matter what the Germans did or said, it would be ill received. If they insisted on the original 'hard' alliance line, they were branded as 'cold warriors' and 'disturbers of the peace'. If they spoke of reunification, this immediately created fears of a too-powerful Germany. At the least sign of rapprochement with Moscow, the spectre of Rapallo was recalled in the world-press. The fact that the West German government could neither pursue an independent foreign policy nor attend to national German interests without criticism, distrust, and enmity from all sides, made the government's position untenable in the long run.

Broadly sketched, this then was the background to the autumn 1966 cabinet crises in Bonn. The goverment's economic policy, which made the crisis more acute, was first and foremost an excuse to topple the government.

The 1966 crisis has been called a 'crisis of leadership', but it was more than that. Erhard's personal lack of resoluteness may perhaps have hastened the crisis, but this was of secondary importance. Sooner or later the crisis would have been unavoidable: it was merely a symptom of the crisis that affected the whole of Western cooperation.

Given the increasing awareness that the FRG's foreign policy line was doomed to failure, the Chancellor's position became weakened and that of the opposition correspondingly strengthened. Any and every defeat for the Federal government in alliance policy meant strength for the 'Gaullist' wing within the coalition, which, headed by Adenauer and Strauss, advocated closer ties with France and a Western European defence organization. Disappointment over reunification policy was, however, the main reason why the minor coalition partner FDP (Free Democratic Party) rebelled in the end. The FDP was neither markedly 'Atlantic' nor 'Gaullist' (in the German sense of the term) but it desired a more independent German policy, including a more flexible attitude towards the GDR and Moscow. For that reason it rejected the German 'Gaullist' solution with respect to Western Europe. The stronger the Gaullist wing within the coalition became, the more difficult did collaboration become for the FDP, until the breakdown on 27th October. And previous elections had shown that cabinet collaboration with the unionist parties CDU and CSU was of no benefit to the FDP.

The autumn 1966 crisis marked an important point in both German and European post-war policy. That alliance policies of the FRG stranded because of inner disagreement meant in practice that the framework for West German policy as a whole was shattered. Not the alliance, but rather domestic West German political forces would decide the course in the future. There was no chance of returning to the old foreign policy line – that would only prolong the crisis. Erhard had held on to the 'Atlantic course' as long as he could; his fall marked the defeat of the original US and Western 'German policy'.

What was now needed was a new foundation for West German policy. The numerous inner clashes and contradictions in Bonn's situation had to be overcome if a stable development were to become possible.

In search of a new strategy

For many years the sole realistic alternative to the 'Atlantic' line in West German foreign policy appeared to be the so-called 'Gaullist' line. Since it is still a conceivable alternative today, we shall deal with it at some length.

The aim was not to make of Europe a military and political unit capable of rivalling the US: rather, what was sought was a Europe that could act as an equal partner with the US in world politics.

Such a solution would seem to remove many of the existing inner contradictions in West German and Western policy. Strategically, a more autonomous West European security organization – in alliance with the US – would offer to West Europeans the advantage that strategy, including nuclear strategy, could be tailor-made to suit West European needs. France would also be able to participate to the full. French and British nuclear forces could one day be combined to form the basis of a force in which West Germany too could take part on an equal footing. The necessary precondition for this, however, would have to be wide-ranging political integration. But even without such German participation in a nuclear force, the security of the FRG would be assured by the identity of interests that would exist between all the West European states. Since Western Europe forms a connected defence area, any attack on the Federal Republic would immediately draw in the other West European countries in defence – that is, if they and not the US had the power of decision-making. The relatively modest power-potential that such a defence organization, in the beginning at least, would represent would not need to mean reduced deterrent capacity vis-à-vis the Soviet Union, for the simple reason that if the US were truly interested in defending Western Europe, it would maintain its nuclear guarantee anyhow.

Nor would such a solution necessarily be disadvantageous for the US. Even if the security interests of Western Europe and the US were not completely identical, and even if a West European union might become an economic rival, it would be hard to imagine a situation where Western Europe could come into truly serious conflict with the US. Shared cultural and political interests dominate the picture. Through defence of their own cultural and political values, Western Europeans would at the same time be defending US interests, also with respect to the Soviet Union.

Even more important than the military aspects would be the fact that West European integration would get a new lease of life. By abolishing the incongruency between economic and military integration, the new line would make possible rapid development towards real political integration. In this would lie the sole possibility for the Federal Republic as a provisory state to achieve a 'true' equal footing, and this in turn would make it easier for West Germans if they should have to accept partition as definite one day.

The establishment of an independent West European defence organization or an integrated West European political union would not necessarily worsen chances of reunification either: on the contrary. What the French view presupposed was indeed a closening of ties within Europe that in the end would enable German reunification to take place. The results of reunification policy would depend on the ability of West German politicians to deal with the East European states. According to this view, these states would no longer need to fear that the FRG would use NATO as a tool to achieve its political ends. The more integrated Western Europe became, the less would it be possible to speak of a West German foreign policy: instead there would be a West European foreign policy, presumably capable of neutralizing any 'aggressive' tendencies in the Federal Republic. And what would be acceptable to the other West European states in the matter of reunification, should also be acceptable to Eastern Europe.

Such an autonomous Western Europe would not necessarily preclude the possibility of a special military status for the FRG, if this would ease the problem of reunification and therefore be desirable for the Germans themselves. Through a gradual normalization of East-West relations, there might even be the possibility of a greater European security system, indeed even political community 'from the Atlantic to the Urals'.

Global power relations seemed in the mid-sixties favourable to a more autonomous arrangement for Western Europe. The two superpowers were then primarily occupied with containing the war in Vietnam and ensuring that it should not affect the situation in Western Europe and thus increase the risk of nuclear war. The danger that such a thing could happen spoke against stronger integration within the Atlantic alliance, especially in the area of nuclear forces. Both the US and the USSR desired stability in Europe. A West European solution that could guarantee a stable development in Europe would be of positive value for both sides.

However, in the end such a 'Gaullist' concept of a West European political community along the lines sketched above had to be abandoned. There were two main reasons: de Gaulle's own ideas differed too greatly from the ideas of West German 'Gaullists' concerning the character of such a community; and the cabinet crises in Bonn created an entirely new situation in West German politics.

As mentioned, de Gaulle saw rapprochement with Eastern Europe as the key to success for a new European policy. He was totally uninterested in any initiatives that might increase tension in Europe. In his view, bilateral contacts were the best approach for overcoming the division of Europe. For that reason, he was not favourable to any wide-ranging institutionalization of West European politics, but hoped that other West European states would follow Paris' line. In practice, this would mean for the FRG that it would have to abandon its established alliance policy as well as the Hallstein doctrine, and instead recognize the existing boundaries. Moreover, even if the FRG would not formally have to recognize the GDR, it would at least have to establish official contacts with East Berlin. All in all, this would mean total renunciation of the old position, in favour of a policy of 'understanding' vis-à-vis East Germany, in the hope that this could one day bring about reunification and equal rights.

An autonomous West European federal union – which, in the era of sharp East-West confrontation might have had a tension-relaxing function by forcing disengagement between the two power-blocs – now risked having a diametrically opposed function, in the French view, and particularly if this political union were built on the principle of equality for its members. Because de Gaulle considered his Ostpolitik to be the only correct line, and because he had no guarantee that it would be adopted by the other partner-states, he gave priority to solution of existing East-West problems instead of insisting on the establishment of a West European union.

The illusory character of the German 'Gaullist' line was due to both the fact that it did not fully agree with de Gaulle's politics, and the fact that the German Gaullists lacked sufficient influence in Bonn in the period to follow. True, the cabinet crisis and change of government meant defeat for the 'Atlanticists', but the victors were the spokesmen of the 'opening towards the East' line. If the Gaullists in the German government had taken over without there being a cabinet crisis and coalition breakdown, the result would probably have been either a policy of 'immobility'[5] or a 'West European' policy under French leadership. Such a government would, because of the strong 'Atlantic' element within the coalition, not have been capable of pursuing an independent policy, but would have had to relinquish to de Gaulle the unchallenged leadership of Western Europe.

With the defeat of the 'Atlanticists', the alternative was suddenly no longer the 'Gaullist' (in the German sense) solution, but a truly West German policy, one which was neither 'anti-American' nor 'anti-Gaullist', but which gave West German national interests priority. Indeed, the Federal Republic had come of age.

Autumn 1966 saw the establishment of the so-called 'Big Coalition' between the Social Democrats (SPD) and the unionist parties (CDU/CSU). This marked the beginnings of a more active West

German foreign policy, where improvement of relations with the East – including the GDR – and with France were major agenda items.

The Kiesinger/Brandt coalition was characterized by inner disagreement on what the goals for this new Ostpolitik should be. A main stumbling-block was how to adjust the FRG's treaty-contractual policy in the German question to these new realities – here primarily Eastern demands for recognition of the status quo and recognition of the GDR as an equal partner.

These demands were presented as an absolute precondition for any form of normalization of relations between West Germany and the East European states, whether on the basis of existing alliances or through an all-European security system. In view of current power-relations in Europe, this standpoint was in fact both realistic and logical. As long as Bonn insisted on toeing the NATO-line, the Warsaw Treaty would also continue to exist, and the two Germanies would continue as equal partners within their respective alliances. Transfer from one alliance to the other was unthinkable for either of them. If normalization should be attempted on such a basis, there was no reason to refuse to recognize the situation as it was: not doing so only served to make normalization more difficult.

On the other hand, should the aim be an all-European system of security, then such recognition would be even more necessary, according to the Eastern view. If Bonn made a point of maintaining alliance ties with the US and with NATO until such time as a solution could be found to the German question; and if it set the establishment of an all-German government as a condition for recognition of the eastern borders, then this would in reality mean that the German Democratic Republic would cease to exist as an autonomous state *before* the Federal Republic withdrew from NATO and *before* Poland's western borders could be recognized by a united Germany. In other words, there would thus be the possibility that the new Germany could refuse to withdraw from NATO and refuse to recognize the Oder-Neisse line – and this would mean a change in power-relations in Europe palpably in Moscow's disfavour. For the Eastern countries to enter into non-aggression pacts with West Germany without legally binding guarantees for the GDR would, in Ulbricht's view, not lessen this danger but in fact increase it.

34

That Ulbricht demanded recognition according to international law of the GDR's existence and of all agreements concerning the GDR and the FRG, however, was not the same as rejecting the idea of possible reunification of the two Germanies. 'Die Vereinigung der deutschen Staaten ist und bleibt unser Ziel', he declared at the SED Congress in April 1967. The condition was that such unification take place within the framework of a European security system to replace the existing alliances.

This all-European line of the GDR and the USSR was no break with their former policy, but simply meant consolidating the GDR's international status and the USSR's political and military position in Europe. However, for Bonn recognition of Eastern demands would mean a radical about-face in foreign and security policy. Until then the Federal Republic had based its entire international role on the treaty basis created through integration into Western cooperation. It was with reference to the Paris Treaties that the FRG had been able to claim national sovereignty and the legitimacy to strive for national union. Further, it was these Treaties that guaranteed its military security. At the same time, however, the Western powers had reserved the right to decide in questions concerning all Germany. Leadership of the West German military forces was placed under joint NATO command. All in all, Bonn's scope for manoeuvring was limited indeed.

The unity that this treaty basis represented, according to Bonn, could not be broken up piecemeal but should, if necessary, be replaced by a new, unified foundation. All the time, the West German government had maintained the official Western view that what was needed was a peace treaty for all Germany. The partition of Germany was seen as a result of the East-West conflict blocking such a peace treaty. Bonn was aware that developments over the years had made reunification through a peace treaty highly unlikely, and that such arguments thus had little force as far as the East was concerned. All the same, Bonn felt that keeping to the original treaty basis would also oblige the Western powers to follow suit, and this would in turn compel them to take German interests into consideration in their policy vis-à-vis the Soviet Union. Above all, it should deter them from recognizing the status quo as a permanent arrangement. Should Bonn have to accept the status quo, this would mean reducing allied motivation for overcoming the partition of Germany and of Europe – and this without any guarantees that such concessions would be honoured by the East.

When it came to the really decisive issues in surmounting the status quo, it was not Bonn but primarily the three Western powers that held the key. True, the West German government might grant legal recognition of the Oder-Neisse border and might recognize the GDR as an equal. But West Germany could not – even had it so wished – take it for granted that the Western powers would agree to the arms control measures which the East set as a condition for normalization in the direction of a European security system. Both sides would have to work actively for this, if there were to be any success. If things stranded here, Bonn would not have come far, while at the same time it would have forfeited the formal basis of legitimacy for reunification demands.

Even if the West German government should remain loyal to the alliance, and even if it assumed that the US and Great Britain would continue to be interested in supporting German unity, it was still not obvious to Bonn why recognition of borders and of the GDR should have any purpose as *unilateral* West German renunciation of mutually-agreed standpoints. If Bonn were to continue to regard the alliance as the means for solving the German question, it was self-evident that any solution would have to take place on a multilaterally agreed basis involving the two superpowers as well. If a solution on this basis were to become anything more than a pure status-quo solution, Bonn presupposed – as did French and East European views – that there should come into being a new European security system. And this would require efforts far more fundamental than merely securing West German recognition of the Oder-Neisse line and of the GDR. Why should not such recognition be seen as part and parcel of a larger comprehensive solution, it seemed reasonable to ask.

In addition to these foreign policy limitations came those connected with domestic affairs. The CDU/CSU-SPD coalition was obliged to build on a whole series of compromises, and this meant in practice that decisions in major foreign policy issues had to be postponed. The coalition partners were in agreement that detente with the East should become the aim of their 'German' policy, seeing detente as the sole feasible way of accomplishing a solution. But opinions differed as to the content of such a policy. This was shown in practice in e.g. the disagreement concerning whether West Germany should be a signatory to the Non-Proliferation Treaty: Brandt was positive, Strauss categorically negative. The whole issue of how far to go in accepting Eastern demands caused dissension. While Brandt expressed understanding of the Polish desire for secure and guaranteed borders, and was willing to recognize the East German government as actual power-wielders in 'the other part of Germany', the CDU/CSU insisted on the principles set out in the Hallstein Doctrine, i.e. that the Bonn government was the sole legitimate spokesman for all Germany, and that recognition of the East German state was thus totally out of the question. The CDU/CSU further maintained that the Oder-Neisse line could not be recognized as a permanent border until such time as there might exist a peace treaty for all Germany.

In this way Bonn's Ostpolitik was ambiguous. And this ambiguity impeded secret negotiations with Moscow in the months prior to the Czechoslovakian crisis.

The military intervention in Czechoslovakia by the five Warsaw Treaty countries on 21 August 1968 marked a vital turning-point in East-West relations in Europe. First of all, the intervention made it clear that the Soviet Union was willing to use force if necessary to stop further disintegration of the Eastern bloc, disintegration which the Soviet government saw as shifting of the balance of power in Europe in its disfavour. For Moscow, progress in the West German anti-status-quo policy, in the form of greater influence in certain Eastern countries, stood as the most important element in this dislocation of power. This was especially true as long as Bonn maintained its close relations with the US while the West still refused to grant concessions on major Soviet security issues in connection with Europe: these issues were of course recognition of borders and of the German Democratic Republic, plus West German adherence to the Non-Proliferation Treaty.

The close ties between West Germany and the United States ruled out any solution of European security issues without US participation. In reality this also ruled out any possibilities of Soviet collaboration with France, in line with the Bucuresti Declaration of 1966. French anti-status-quo policy was based on the assumption of West

European autonomy vis-à-vis the US and opened the possibility of such collaboration, even though it was also directed against the dominant Soviet influence in other East European countries. This policy would not necessarily imply a dislocation of power to the disfavour of the Soviet Union.

France had encouraged West Germany's Ostpolitik. But when rapprochement towards the East had come so far that Moscow would no longer accept it without Western concessions, and these concessions – which were dependent on Bonn – were not forthcoming, this meant that France's Ostpolitik was blocked. Moscow had no possibilities of shutting the door on West German Ostpolitik while keeping it open for France, so long as these two countries officially supported each other in their Eastern policy. The intervention in Czechoslovakia meant that neither Paris nor Bonn could continue as before.

The Czechoslovakian crisis revealed how West Germany's importance for East-West relations and indeed for the entire European situation was fast increasing. This fact had long been ignored, not least because Bonn had refrained from taking any political initiatives that might be interpreted as attempts to break away from the Western treaty basis. After the intervention in Czechoslovakia, the need for a clearer demarcation of West German standpoints became apparent. Both US, Soviet, and French policies towards Europe were dependent on which line Bonn was to follow. Only when Bonn had made known its views could it be possible to define the role of the alliance and the bases for East-West policy for the future. Until the Czechoslovakian crisis, both Soviet and French policy had assumed not only that West Germany would grant important concessions in the German question, but also that the Federal Republic would distance itself from the US and accept Paris and Moscow as major actors in the regulation of European security. Actual events, however, were to take a different direction.

First of all, the West German government gave unconditional reassurances of its will to continue the policy of detente towards the East, and this time with the main emphasis on Moscow in order to avoid creating new tensions. Secondly, West Germany stated that it considered the continued existence and indeed the strengthening of NATO to be an absolute condition. Thirdly, it soon became clear that no significant changes would take place in Bonn's views on major conflict issues on the East-West conflict as long as the governmental coalition continued. While one of the coalition partners – the SPD – indicated that these questions would be regulated in a way acceptable to the East within an all-European peace arrangement, indeed basing its entire *Europapolitik* on such a solution, the CDU/SCU leadership on the other hand interpreted Soviet policy as expressed in connection with Czechoslovakia as 'die totale Absage Moskaus an die Bonner Bemühungen um die Wiedervereinigung', and placed the main emphasis on strengthening West European and Western cooperation.[6]

Viewed together, these standpoints – detente on the basis of NATO and with an all-European peace arrangement as the goal – reveal that what in practice was excluded was further continuation of the French all-European line, since this presupposed that West Germany should distance itself from US and NATO cooperation. Likewise, possibilities for a French-Soviet dialogue on the solution of European security problems were no longer realistic. As long as West Germany maintained its US and NATO ties, Bonn and Washington would remain the major negotiating partners with Moscow in these matters – and not Paris. An all-European security system or peace arrangement would thus be possible solely on the basis of close collaboration with the United States.

A further consequence of major long-range importance for European politics lay implicit in the West German stand: the fact that NATO was to be kept intact until an all-European peace arrangement might be able to replace the alliance, and that in addition Bonn saw a clear connection between the establishment of such a peace arrangement and the concessions demanded of West Germany, made it apparent that Bonn would occupy a key position in any negotiations on these issues. As the strongest European NATO partner and as the decisive Western actor in the question of an all-European security system, West Germany would have to *demonstrate* that it was the leading West European state in the most vital areas of foreign and security policy, and not least integration policy, if its line were to have any chances whatsoever of realization. The question of establishing an all-European security system could not be looked at in isolation from either Atlantic or West European integration. And to be able to stand forth as a negotiating partner vis-à-vis the Soviet Union concerning all-European issues, West Germany would have to prove that it had the mandate to act on behalf of both NATO and Western Europe. In addition, of course, it would have to prove to the Soviet Union that such a line could be compatible with Soviet interests.

The first question to be clarified was whether Bonn could obtain the necessary mandate from the West. This matter was connected with the future role of NATO in European politics as well as with the political and economic organization of Western Europe. The conflict between the British and French views had to be solved: this was a conflict in which relations with the US and East-West relations in Europe played a central role, but which was increasingly being determined by concrete integration developments within the European Community.

III. West German policy in an all-European perspective

The change in the international system that came about as a result of the Czechoslovakian crisis in 1968 and the formation of the new social-liberal coalition in Bonn in the autumn of 1969 marked the start of a new phase in West German and in European politics. Up till then, detente had avoided the more fundamental political conflict-issues in East West relations, i.e. those connected with Central Europe and the German question.

It was now that the real era of Ostpolitik began to take shape as a coherent policy defining the German national question, EC integration, alliance policy, and East-West relations as mutually interdependent parts of one and the same concept. The foundation created through this policy is still, at the close of the 1970s, the official view – not only for Bonn's own Ostpolitik but for policy on Germany and on East-West relations in general, including the negotiations in the Conference of Security and Cooperation in Europe (CSCE). All this has meant a fundamental re-orientation of West German policy, together with 'Europeanization' of the German question.

Since these issues are central to our study, we shall here sketch the various components involved, and their placement in relation to each other. While Ostpolitik may in recent years have lost some of its dynamics, it is nonetheless important for Bonn. And, as we have already mentioned, Bonn today has greater resources and greater manoeuvring space than before. There is therefore good reason to assume that the legitimacy to further national West German interests that has been granted the FRG through the new multilaterally approved policies concerning Germany and Europe will not be given up, except in connection with fairly dramatic events. Equally important for continuity, however, are also the substantial increases in cooperation and collaboration with other countries. Here we are thinking primarily of collaboration with France, both bilateral and within the EC, but also of practical political ties that have been established with the East, including the GDR. In the following pages we shall deal with the major features in the amplification of this new foundation for West Germany's *Europapolitik*.

Bonn – Paris: long-range interplay on European policy

At the French – West German summit conference held in Paris, on 13 March 1969, the importance of the changed situation and its relevance for relations between the two countries was discussed and a kind of compromise reached. In reality this meant that France temporarily agreed to accommodate its EC policy to the West German Ostpolitik line, in return for West German assurances that the aim was to be an 'autonomous Europe'. De Gaulle declared that the question of further development of the EC was primarily dependent on West Germany. Although France gave priority to consolidating and strengthening the Community, if others considered an extension now important, France would not oppose re-organization of the EC with this in mind. De Gaulle further made it clear that France would acknowledge West Germany's right to continue to build its Ostpolitik on the basis of NATO membership and the continued presence of US forces in Central Europe, as long as considerations of security so dictated. France herself, however, would not return to integration within NATO, he stated.

The consequence to be drawn from de Gaulle's recognition of West German NATO policy was that it would be Bonn and Washington that led negotiations with Moscow: in other words, that de Gaulle accepted that these two and not France should take the lead in Ostpolitik – for the time being at least.

It was now left to Bonn itself to determine which course West Germany should follow. From the point of view of France, it was important that this course should be marked in a binding and long-term way. In response to such expectations, the West German government actively tried to clarify its policies, both with respect to French-German relations, the EC, the alliance, and Ostpolitik. Some main lines were drawn up by Chancellor Kurt Georg Kiesinger immediately upon his return from the summit meeting in Paris:

We both [i.e. France and West Germany] wish to create an autonomous Europe – this is impotant. We want to create such an autonomous Europe, but we are thinking also beyond the borders of such a Western Europe, looking eastwards, in order to establish better relations with the East. Whether this can ever lead to the formation of a great Europe extending from one side to the other – this must remain an open question, a distant dream. In the first round what is important is to organize Western Europe, at the same time trying to arrange matters with the East in a more satisfactory way.[7]

Bonn emphasized unequivocally its interest in intensifying the expansion of the EC, hoping to make of the Community a cornerstone for its entire European policy. Also in the matter of institutional framework Bonn's support of the French-inspired intergovernmental line became apparent – with the main emphasis on political collaboration on the governmental level. However, while the supranational element was played down somewhat, there was never any question of accepting a political 'dilution' of the Community to enable further expansion to take place. On the contrary, it was seen as necessary to strengthen foreign policy collaboration with the aim of gradually achieving solidary conduct in world policy.

Bonn's new course showed that the foundation for close French-West German cooperation within the EC existed, also with respect to relations with other countries. The general unanimity between the two countries and the long-terms aims of European policy were heavily emphasized at the summit meeting held in January 1970 between Chancellor Willy Brandt and President Georges Pompidou. Here Brandt declared that relations between France and the Federal Republic had entered into a new phase, one no longer characterized by rapprochement but 'by an almost self-evident feeling of the need to stand together'. The 1963 agreement on collaboration was given increased meaning by both sides, also with regard to security policy. And this represented a new element in Bonn's line of argument.

The platform of the Hague Meeting

Interestingly and importantly, while France's policy of independence as to NATO had given rise to fears that political strengthening of the EC might lead to dissolution of the Western defence alliance, West Germany's new and more active role – viewed against the background of the reliability of West German NATO support – did *not* lead to such unease, even though the actual content of West German policy here was in the main identical to the earlier French line. Strengthened political collaboration within the EC, combined with close coordination of West German and US policy on issues of security vis-à-vis the Eastern states (of course under NATO auspices) now seemed infinitely less risky for the other EC countries than would cooperation without US approval.

This is probably one of the main reasons why the EC unanimously supported the idea of a summit meeting aimed to accelerate development of the Community, including ways of dealing with EC extension and foreign policy coordination. Given such support, it is understandable that the summit meeting – held at the Hague on 1st-2nd December 1969 – meant a real breakthrough in integration efforts as well as in Bonn's entire *Europapolitik*.

West Germany's aims for Europe

Here we shall briefly sketch some of the ideas that, since the formation of the social-liberal coalition government in the FRG, have become fairly permanent components of West Germany's *Europapolitik* with respect to long-term organization of political cooperation in Europe and the solution of certain central political problems. What characterizes the policies of this government in contrast with the Big Coalition and earlier West German governmental policy is the fact that it has been formulated as a logical unity, where realization of goals in one area need not take place at the expense of goals in other areas. Security and integration policy, for instance, are linked with the politics of the unsolved national German question, but in a way that does not demand capitulation of the opposing party. This had of course been the case with earlier policy in this area: now the aim is to build on the community of interests existing between all parties involved, in order to solve political problems in a satisfactory manner. Since the one area is seen as irrevocably interlinked with the other, it is difficult to speak of any absolute gradation of priorities and aims in West German policy. All the same, it seems reasonable to begin with the German question, since integration and security – including Ostpolitik – are mentioned by Bonn itself as factors instrumental in resolving this issue.

Policy in the 'German question' has often been summarized by Bonn as aiming to maintain and make possible 'the German option'. National reunification as a 'once and for all' action is definitely out of the question. What is held open is the option for possible national unity as a long-term goal.

While still Foreign Minister, Walter Scheel explained this in the following way, which still holds good today:

> We do not allow anyone to require of us that we shall abandon the political goal of bringing the German people together again. The German option is an irrepudiable aim of our policy.[8]

The goal is not necessarily unity as a state. The form would have to be decided within the framework of security policy. Rather, the aim is to create a European peace system in which Germans from both the German states may themselves decide how the national community should be organized. According to Brandt, this should also be possible 'in the form of a special relationship between the two state organizations that have developed'. Brandt also emphasized the connection between rapprochement between the two German states and East-West rapprochement in general.

> Only all-European rapprochement can and will result in the two parts of Germany being able to come closer together . . . There exists no other road to national unity.[9]

The fact that West Germany's policy aims at solving the German question within the framework of an all-European peace settlement raises the question of how such a peace settlement relates, in Bonn's view, to West European integration policy. The most important thing that can be ascertained here is that the West German government considers strengthening the EC and West European cooperation in general to be a necessary precondition for rapprochement with the East. This has clearly been demonstrated through West Germany's active contributions to putting resolutions from the Hague summit meeting into practice. In the view of the West German government, an expanded and strengthened European Community is to be a major component of the more comprehensive European peace settlement. Bonn wishes to have the support of as much as possible of Western Europe in its attempts to improve relations eastwards – both in order to strengthen its own negotiating position and in order not to risk becoming politically isolated. In this connection, the procedure for political coordination followed within EC circles is seen as highly important as a means of training for achieving a necessary 'European solidarity of interests'. Here the perspectives for Bonn are identical to those for Paris: ever-increasing integration under a confederative organizational form which permits maintenance of formal state sovereignty. This would provide increased concord and solidarity while still keeping outward flexibility, so that the Community would not be heavily characterized by bloc-formation. Here of course considerations concerning the wish for East-West rapprochement enter into the picture.

The West German government has not indicated any limits in principle as to how far EC ingration might be carried without coming into conflict with the maintenance of formal state sovereignty, except for a statement by Brandt:

> Also in a European peace arrangement national components will keep their rank.[10]

The establishment of a federation is not considered realistic within the foreseeable future.

Obviously, this all-European perspective on EC expansion, including collaboration between the EC and neutral countries, presupposes a decrease in bloc confrontation in Europe in such a way that the perspective can be accepted by the East as well. Otherwise, the whole all-European perspective would be meaningless. An important question is thus how Bonn imagines the bloc system being replaced by a cooperative system – especially as concerns the role of the alliances. Again and again, West Germany has reiterated its stand: the Federal Republic will build on alliance solidarity in the transition phase towards a permanent peace system for all of

Europe. As Foreign Minister in the Big Coalition, Willy Brandt had expressed this clearly:

> Anyone with any sense of realism will know that in the foreseeable future we can find our security only within the Atlantic defence alliance, and that this is also the best foundation on which we may continue our struggles for decrease in tensions and a solution to the German question.[11]

In his 'State of the Nation' speech of 14 January 1970, Brandt repeated this stand in the now famous formulation: 'Die Bundesrepublik Deutschland ist kein «Wanderer zwischen zwei Welten»'.

However, it is also apparent from statements by Brandt and other members of the government that the alliance is not considered eternal: rather, it is seen as a necessity until such time as agreement can be achieved concerning an all-European peace system. Brandt says:

> A strong and solidary alliance is necessary, until the processes in connection with overcoming East-West disagreements have been completed and an effective all-European security system has been established, guaranteeing security and freedom of action to all European nations.[12]

In speaking of the Atlantic alliance, what Brandt is mainly thinking about is clearly relations between Western Europe and the US. His view of power-relations is such that he considers the US presence in Western Europe to be a continued necessity. However, according to the official West German view, the alliance and the US engagement exist to serve a purpose: that of helping to create the basis for negotiations with the Soviet Union and other East European states on solving security problems in Europe, in hopes of decreasing bloc tensions. A final solution to the problems of European security is possible only within the framework of an all-European arrangement to replace the alliances:

> It is obvious that a satisfactory solution to Europe's security problems is to be found only within the framework of a European peace system.[13]

47

A necessary precondition for the creation of a balanced all-European system that would render the alliances superflous is, in Brandt's opinion, that West European cooperation be sufficiently strengthened:

> I consider the unification of Western Europe to be an all-European task and – with a view to overcoming East-West antagonisms – as an indispensable extension of the goals of the North Atlantic alliance.[14]

An equally important precondition is that both parties to the East-West confrontation should be willing to carry out balanced force reductions in Europe. This aim has been a central element in West German politics ever since the NATO ministerial council meeting in Reykjavik, spring 1968. The 'signal from Reykjavik' has been repeated and intensified on several later occasions within the framework of the MBFR negotiations. The West German government considers the need for US military presence in Western Europe to be directly related to the extent to which mutual and balanced force reductions can be achieved. If both sides can agree to such reductions, US military withdrawal from Europe can take place without disturbing the balance of power, and without weakening the reliability of the US security guarantee. Chancellor Helmut Schmidt, during his time as Minister of Defence, underlined the political importance of such mutual de-escalation:

> Here it is important that we view the question of mutual force reductions not only in a narrow military perspective, but that we also see it as a political task. If it succeeds, the Americans will be able to leave Western Europe without losing it, and this under circumstances that would make it improbable that they would have to return later to head off a threatening danger. The withdrawal of US troops should not be seen as retreat, but indeed as a contribution to cooperation and de-escalation of confrontation in Europe.[15]

These then were the major features of the underlying concepts on which the social-liberal coalition based its Ostpolitik. As we have seen, it was in part a question of very long-term goals which – if they can be realized – will have wide-ranging consequences for all of Europe, and globally as well.

The Eastern Treaties: another foundation of Bonn's European policy

The underlying plan to the negotiations with the East was defined by the West German government as being 'a unified whole' aimed at getting all parts of the above-mentioned concept of Europe to fit together. Bonn considered it necessary that any and every new initiative in the German question and in Ostpolitik should take place on the basis of the existing legal treaty framework, particularly with reference to the four-power special responbility for Germany as a whole. This meant that no agreements or treaties that Bonn might enter into with the East might be allowed to prejudice a peace treaty for Germany, nor might it annul or limit the formal responsibilities and duties of the four great powers.

In addition to these legal contractual considerations in connection with the German question, Bonn also had to keep in mind current international constellations of interest. This required continual coordination all along the line, at every step of the negotiating process. It was considered as especially important that the FRG should be covered from the rear during negotiations, i.e. that West Germany should have a kind of mandate to act on behalf of the entire West.

The situation was in fact similar within the Warsaw Treaty Organization and COMECON. Bonn's prime counterpart in negotiations was here Moscow, and Moscow placed great emphasis on maintaing the cohesion of the internal Eastern alliance, and that this should form the basis for efforts at rapprochement. This was in line with the 'Breshnev Doctrine' of 26 September 1968, which asserted that the sovereignty and right of self-determination of the socialist countries were to be subordinated to the principle of the indivisibility of the socialist community and mutual defence obligations.

Parallel with negotiations between West Germany and the Eastern countries, the superpowers were conducting their bilateral negotiations on the possibilties of strategic arms control (SALT) and mutual and balanced force reductions in Central Europe (MBFR). Should any major changes take place in German policy, these would have to be accommodated into the superpowers' strategic planning and into East-West relations in general. In order to understand the importance of the *Grundlagenvertrag* and inter-German developments as a whole, one must bear in mind all these interrelated points. The many negotiations and agreements undertaken should be viewed as an entity. The negotiating parties sought to link the points together by deliberately making concessions in one area dependent on reciprocal concessions in another. The stated aim was to bring all parts together into a unified solution which could serve as a point of departure for a new system of security in Europe.

A brief survey of negotiations in the period 1970-1973 will help to illustrate this. The major 'package deal' represented by the final round of negotiations still forms the sole mutually accepted basis of East-West rapprochement in Europe.

The Moscow Treaty of 12 August 1970 marked an important breakthrough. It complied with the main demands of both sides: Moscow's demands for recognition of the status quo in Europe, including the border question and the GDR as a sovereign state; and Bonn's demands for practical-political rapprochement possibilities which could in the long run help to bring the two Germanies closer within the framework of a European security arrangement. Such dualism also characterizes the remaining agreements, including the final statement of the CSCE in Helsinki: recognition of the status quo as a point of departure for a policy of rapprochement with possibilities of overcoming the status quo at a later, unspecified date.

To avoid the risk of freezing the status quo, the Western powers and Bonn set as a condition for ratification of the Moscow Treaty and also the Warsaw Treaty (7 December 1970) that the position of West Berlin should be assured in a manner that made continuation and expansion of relations with West Germany possible.

Moscow, on the other hand, made such a Berlin solution contingent on Western support of the proposal to hold a European conference on security and cooperation. In other words, the idea was that the questions of Berlin and all Germany, as well as East-West rapprochement in general, should be accommodated into a contractual framework which also gave the Soviet Union some possibilities of exercising control.

However, it was precisely this Soviet desire for control possibilities that intensified the Western need to ensure against a situation where such control could be exerted unilaterally and arbitrarily. In return for the Soviet gambit in the CSCE, Bonn and the Western powers set two more conditions, in addition to the Berlin solution. First, that relations between the two German states should be contractually agreed upon in advance; and that the conference on security and cooperation in Europe be thoroughly prepared.

This placed the Berlin question in the centre of interest. If negotiations were to continue, indeed if rapprochement were not to be blocked, formal consent was needed from the four powers who were still responsible for 'Germany as a whole'. On 25 February 1971, President Nixon made finding a solution to the Berlin question a condition for MBFR negotiations as well. After Soviet party leader Breshnev had, in a speech of 14 May in Tiflis the same year, supported the idea of mutual and balanced force reductions in Europe, and after progress was also achieved in SALT, Berlin approached a solution as well. On 3 September 1971 the four-power agreement on Berlin was provisorily signed by ambassadors of the four countries.

The agreement provided for a contractually based assurance of West Berlin's position. From the West German point of view it was important that 'relations between the Western sector in Berlin and the Federal Republic of Germany (could) be maintained and developed', even though it was also stated that 'these sectors, in the same way as previously, are not part of the Federal Republic of Germany and shall not be governed by it in the future either'. The treaty contained authorization for the two German states and West Berlin to work out arrangements concerning transit traffic to West Berlin and concerning visits etc. between West Berlin and the German Democratic Republic. Agreements on these matters were signed on 17 and 20 December 1971 respectively.

The parties still had retreat options, however. Bonn had not yet ratified the Moscow and Warsaw Treaties, nor had the four great powers given final signatures to the Berlin Agreement. First they wanted closer clarification of future relations between the two German states. The Soviet Union further declared that the Berlin Agreement would not enter into force until the Treaties with Bonn had been ratified. Bonn wanted a general agreement with the GDR before ratifying the 'Eastern Treaties', but the GDR was not willing to bind itself until ratification was in order.

On 18 April 1972, however, the East German party leader Erich Honecker made a statement in Sofia that helped to ease the ratification process in Bonn. He declared that the GDR was ready, as soon as ratification had taken place, to begin an exchange of views on normalization of relations with the Federal Republic. 'This could become the start of a development – I should like to repeat – leading to peaceful *Nebeneinander* between the GDR and the FRG, to normal good neighbourly relations aimed at a *Miteinander* in the interests of peace, in the interests of the citizens of both states'. The key-words here had originally been formulated by Brandt.

The final compromise as regards procedure went as follows: a limited agreement – the so-called 'traffic agreement' – was formulated between the two German states in the form of a draft treaty before Bonn ratified the Eastern Treaties on 17 May 1972. The traffic agreement was signed on 26 May. Then followed the final signing of the Berlin Agreements by the four powers, to enter into force on 3 June 1972. By then the first SALT agreement had also been reached – on 26 May 1972. And the NATO countries had in a meeting of 31 May 1972 declared themselves ready to begin preparation for the Conference on Security and Cooperation in Europe. After this the way was open for direct negotiations between Bonn and East Berlin concerning the basic treaty (*Grundlagenvertrag*). Secretaries of State Bahr (FRG) and Kohl (GDR) began 'exchanges of views' on 15 July; as of 16 August these exchanges received status as official negotiations. By 8 November the agreement was ready for counter-signing, and final signing of the treaty took place in Berlin on 21 December 1972.

Between the countersigning and final signing of the 'Treaty on the basis of relations between the GDR and the FRG' (*Grundlagenvertrag*) there were federal elections in West Germany. The elections were held a year ahead of schedule, owing to the precarious parliamentary situation that had arisen in the Bundestag over the ratification issue. Controversy on the Eastern Treaties led to the SPD/FDP coalition losing its narrow majority in the Bundestag, when some of its representatives joined the opposition in late April 1972. That ratification could take place after all was due to the fact that the opposition abstained from voting. It was now obvious that the government could scarcely continue on such a parliamentary basis. In the election campaign that followed, the government made its

Ostpolitik the major issue, wanting both voter approval of what had been achieved and a mandate to continue further along the same lines. Bundestag elections of 19 November that year provided a convincing victory for the Brandt/Scheel government, which could now safely proceed to sign the basic agreement with the GDR.

The most critical phase in bilateral negotiations between West Germany and the Eastern countries was now over. The *Grundlagenvertrag* was ratified in Bonn on 11 May and in East Berlin on 13 June 1973, entering into force as of 21 June that year. On 12 June and 15 June, respectively, the GDR and the FRG applied for UN membership; and on 18 September 1973 both German states were received into the United Nation as full members of equal standing.

There still remained a few legal problems before a normalization agreement could be signed between the Federal Republic and Czechoslovakia on 11 December 1973. That over, all barriers had now been removed that had previously stood in the way of establishing normal diplomatic relations between the Federal Republic and the Eastern countries, and between the German Democratic Republic and the West. Moreover, the way was open for both states to participate on an equal footing in CSCE and MBFR negotions. The *Grundlagenvertrag* between the FRG and the GDR was concluded between formally sovereign and equal states. This meant that Bonn definitively abandoned the 'Hallstein Doctrine' (sole representation rights); and in practice this was to mean that the number of countries with which the German Democratic Republic had diplomatic relations increased from 32 to over 100 in the course of a few months. The borders between the two German states were recognized as state borders in international law. Relations between them were to build on the principles of equality and non-interference in each other's domestic affairs. Furthermore, in relations between themselves as well as with third parties, the FRG and GDR pledged that they would renounce the use of violence or any threat thereof, and respect existing borders and the sovereignty and territorial integrity of all states. They also promised to support work aimed at promoting security and cooperation in Europe, and efforts to achieve general and complete disarmament under effective international control.

Considering the unequal points of departure of the two German states, one might feel that the final results go rather strongly in favour of the GDR. After all, the Democratic Republic achieved international recognition and legal determination of its existing borders, whereas the gains for Bonn were not tangibly demonstrable, except in the form of international good will obtained. However, it should also be kept in mind that the two parties had different goals. Whereas the GDR was primarily interested in gaining equal status and guaranteeing what had already been achieved, Bonn's main goal was to lay the foundation for long-term rapprochement. Most of the GDR's demands were such that they could be fulfilled through the treaty itself. West German demands were more concerned with future possibilities: and the extent to which they could be fulfilled would depend on further developments and relations between the parties, as well as on East-West relations in general. As far as Bonn was concerned, the main thing was that the way should be opened for normalization and rapprochement on the concrete level, and that it should legitimize efforts towards a peace settlement for Europe 'where the German people in free self-determination may regain their unity', as formulated in the 'Letter on German Unity' which was, at Bonn's request, attached to the agreement as a separate document.

In addition to symbolic concessions – e.g. that East Berlin accepted Bonn's letter on 'German unity' and further agreed to the use of the term 'permanent representation' rather than 'diplomatic representation' (Bonn justified this by saying the term was intended to show that relations were something *more* than what was usual and normal between states) – it was also unequivocally stated that the agreement aimed at linking the two states closer in various practical-political areas. Paragraph 7 is central here:

The Federal Republic of Germany and the German Democratic Republic declare themselves prepared to arrange practical and humanitarian questions as normalization of relations between the two progresses ('im Zug der Normaliserung ihrer Beziehungen'). On the basis of the present agreement and for mutual advantage they will conclude agreements to develop and promote cooperation within the fields of trade and commerce, science and technology, communications, legal accounts outstanding, post and telegraph services, health services, culture, sports, environmental protection and in other fields.

In a joint communiqué issued in connection with the signing of the agreement, both parties support a regular system of political consultations: 'Both governments agreed that they, as normalization ... progresses, will consult with each other on matters of joint interest, particularly such as may be of importance for assuring peace in Europe'.

The key phrase in all of this is 'im Zug der Normalisierung'. It makes it clear that rapprochement between the two German states will be contingent on East-West developments in Europe as a whole.

The Federal Republic's official stand on the German question after the Eastern Treaties

For Bonn, the legal basis of the German question has always played an essential role in the formulation of foreign, security, and integration policies. Since the *Grundlagenvertrag* of 21 December 1972 represents a 'rounding off' of Ostpolitik agreements, it seems reasonable to expect that the official West German interpretation of the importance of this treaty will also influence Bonn's future German policy, and thereby its European policy as well. This should be emphasized, not least because the 1972 Treaty is not something that has been forced upon the Federal Republic by the Four Powers: rather, it is the result of negotiations conducted by Bonn itself. The Eastern Treaties reflect Bonn's own accommodation in the German question, how Bonn has fitted them into the realities of the current international situation. To the extent that Bonn pursues an active German policy and Ostpolitik in the future, there seems to be reason to assume that this will take place on the foundation provided by the *Grundlagenvertrag*. This treaty may in fact be considered as the official West German view of policy in the German question. It fits quite unambiguously into the earlier mentioned all-European perspective.

In the following we shall limit ourselves to a brief survey of the legal aspects of the new Treaty as expressed by the West German side. Later we return to the question of putting this policy into practice, in the light of internal and external conditions.

The *Grundlagenvertrag* of 21 December 1972 provides – according to the ruling of the Federal Constitution Court of the FRG, 31 July 1973 – the necessary foundation for rapprochement between the two German states, and can therefore *not* be said to conflict with the West German Constitution's 'reunification command' – i.e. that the West German authorities have an obligation to work actively for German reunification and to prevent any steps being taken that might impede such efforts. Nor does it – according to the Court – affect article 7 of the German Treaty of 1954, which states that the three Western powers shall support Bonn's efforts to achieve a re-united Germany with a free democratic constitution of the same type as that of the Federal Republic. The Court has determined that, just as before, the government of the FRG has every right in any international situation – including vis-à-vis the GDR – to 'support state unity for the German people through free self-determination, and in its policies attempt to achieve this aim by peaceful means and in agreement with the general principles of international law'. This is made more concrete by the statement that the Treaty 'may be the first step in a longer process, which to begin with may result in one of the variants of confederation known to international law, i.e. a step in the direction of the reunification of the German people in one state: in other word, in the direction of a re-organization of Germany'.[16]

This verdict, considered as valid West German state law and binding on the political authorities, builds on the argumentation that the *Grundlagenvertrag* is in fact a bilateral agreement between two states, and as such subject to the rules of international law; on the other hand, it concerns the special relationship between the two parts of a Germany still existing, albeit incapable of action. It thus has a 'dual character': in 'kind' it is an international legal agreement; by 'specific content' an agreement regulating 'inter-se' relations. It does not represent 'any final solution of the German question'.[17]

On the other hand, nor is the treaty a 'transitional solution' to be replaced by other agreements. With reference to its very title *'Grundlagenvertrag'*, it is emphasized that the treaty is 'a new basis for arranging relations between the two states', a basis on which the two states themselves may decide to build. In other words, the treaty may form the basis for a gradual new arrangement of inter-German relations although the character or concrete content of such a new arrangement cannot be deduced from the treaty as it now stands. This may take place gradually through the 'legal concrete measures' which will necessarily be carried out. Or it may happen through more fundamental changes to which both parties would agree, including revisions of the Basic Treaty itself – provided that such changes are in keeping with the basic principles of the treaty.[18]

The court considers it of vital importance that the Basic Treaty should also be legally evaluated in connection with the overall detente policy of the West German government. It declares: 'In this connection the *Grundlagenvertrag* becomes of the same fundamental importance as the Moscow and Warsaw Treaties'. This is set out in a manner that should be taken into consideration in regard to the question of Bonn's future orientation to the German question. The Court states:

> It (*Grundlagenvertrag*) is not a step that may be 'corrected' at will, as frequently happens with many steps in politics. Rather, it forms, as the title indicates, the basis of a long-term new politics. For that reason, it contains neither time-limits nor provisions for termination. It represents an historical turning-point which shall form the basis for a re-organization of relations between the Federal Republic of Germany and the German Democratic Republic.[19]

In stating that the *Grundlagenvertrag* forms a fundamental part of the FRG's contractual foundations in the German question with respect to both the four-power responsibility for Germany 'as a whole' and the German Treaty of 1954, as well as to the Moscow and Warsaw Treaties of 1970, and by declaring that it is in keeping with the 'reunification command' of the Federal German Constitution, Bonn has not only created for itself a platform for pursuing a deliberate German policy. It has also taken upon itself the constitutional duty to do so, within the larger European framework of the Eastern Treaties. Since the Basic Treaty is so formulated that it is up to the two German states to make concrete the further development of closer mutual relations, the possibility is left open for bilateral rapprochement, should the multilateral approach fail.

When one bears in mind West Germany's rise to prominence as the leading nation in Western Europe, ranking also as a global actor, this state of affairs may be of long-range importance. It would be beyond the scope of the present work to go into closer detail concerning the importance of the Eastern Treaties for the legal foundations of the German question. As a rather neutral summary of current West German 'doctrine' in this area we may mention that it covers:

- insistence on the stand that the Federal Republic is part of a not yet re-organized Germany, and that the FRG represents *this* Germany, whereas it does not represent the GDR;
- maintenance of four-power responsibility for all Germany, including Berlin;
- maintenance of the Paris Treaty of 1954;
- the demand that West German policies concerning Germany shall be in keeping with the Constitution, including the 're-unification command';
- recognition of the GDR as a sovereign and equal partner both in bilateral relations between the two German states and in relations with third parties;
- a distinction between national and international legal recognition: the GDR is not recognized in terms of diplomacy and international law, but in terms of state law; 'special relations' between the two German states of non-international legal character and aimed at further rapprochement on the foundations laid by the Basic Treaty of 21 December 1972.
- express linkage of the Basic Treaty with the Moscow and Warsaw Treaties of 1970, including recognition of the existing borders (which may be altered only by peaceful means), the principle of non-aggression – in other words, all the vital CSCE principles.

This contractual basis of Bonn's policies in the German question contains a few mutually conflicting points. Some of the old elements do not harmonize with the new, as exemplified by the insistence on maintaining the 1954 Treaty. Reunification through the alliance and according to 'Western' pattern conflicts not only with what seems realistic, but also with the principles of equality, non-intervention, etc. set out in the Basic Treaty. Why then should the FRG insist on maintaining the 1954 Treaty? Mainly because if one were to depart in any way from the principle that conclusion of the Eastern Treaties was not to affect existing contractual obligations, this might unleash a flood of demands for countless new revisions. Historical experience when it comes to Art. 7 of the 1954 Treaty is important here: it had never been politically utilized in East-West relations expect as a means to tie Bonn to a status-quo, Western line. Hans-Petter Schwarz therefore expresses a widespread opinion in stating that what has taken place is 'an erosion of the political content' in this obligation, and that Art. 7 'no longer is a decisive instrument for active politics'.[20] In practice it is a dead letter. The only thing that could breathe new life into Art. 7 would probably be a new version of Western 'policy of strength'.

The all-European perspective: preconditions and consequences on the international systems level

The multilateralization and Europeanization of Bonn's policy on Germany which Brandt's government had stressed, and which made its imprints on the final act of the CSCE, was meant to combine various aspects of West German foreign and security policy into one unified concept. Whether this line will be followed up depends of course not only on West Germany itself, but also on a whole series of circumstances partially or wholly outside the reach of Bonn: superpower relations, developments in the EC, alliance policy, etc. The matter at stake is in fact what may be termed the 'CSCE perspective', and this presupposes coordination and balancing of interests over a broad spectrum and on various levels. Indeed, when one considers the complexity and scope of this process, what is remarkable is that it has not encountered even greater obstacles or shown signs of stagnation on more points than has been the case to date: the process is still going on, albeit somewhat slowly.

In evaluating the developmental possibilities of West German foreign policy and security policy, it seems both defensible and fruitful to take precisely this 'CSCE perspective' as a point of departure. However, if we were to attempt an even partly thorough discussion of the practicability of this concept, far more time and space would be needed than is available within the present framework. In the following, we permit ourselves a leap in the empirical analysis: we shall concentrate on those areas that have, in recent years, proved most critical as concerns the realization of West German *Europapolitik*. These are the areas of superpower relations, the development of the European Community, and relations between the Federal Republic and the United States. By thus limiting ourselves, we hope to clarify more exactly what it is that makes these areas so important here.

Identification and discussion of the preconditions for and probable consequences of the realization of an all-European perspective should provide us with a better foundation for later analysis of alternatives. Thus, we shall start by analysing a hypothetical development based on the assumption that Bonn will follow up its Ostpolitik along the lines we have already indicated. This in turn presupposes that both superpowers (and other European powers as well) are willing to adjust their policies in a manner compatible both with Bonn's Ostpolitik and with the aforementioned EC developments.

After this portion of the analysis, we shall discuss the extent to which these assumptions seem reasonable in view of current political realities. We shall then take up the question of possible alternatives. Here we will have the advantage of being able to draw on the insights gained in the survey presented in the preceding analysis, where we dealt with actual and potential points of conflict, coinciding and conflicting interests in connection with the all-European perspective.

As already mentioned, West Germany's conception of 'Europe' presupposes that West German policy on Germany and in the area of Ostpolitk can be coordinated with policies of the other EC countries into a more integrated whole. Through increasingly more binding joint policies outwards, the EC is gradually to achieve greater autonomy in international affairs – also vis-à-vis the United States. The idea is to maintain cooperation within NATO as well, all the while seeing this as a necessity with regard to the military balance of power in Europe. But inherent in this conception is the idea that in the long run the EC shall take over more and more responsibility for security policy, as organized cooperation and expanded community of interests with the East lend to security policy a stronger non-military character. Developing the EC as a balancing element in East-West relations, together with proposals for mutual and balanced force reductions in Central Europe, form the two main foundations of West Germany's Ostpolitik.

If the European Community is to have such a balancing role in

East-West relations, however, this will require a great deal in the way of policy coordination – not only within the EC itself, but also between the EC and the US, and not least between the two super-powers. In fact, the interests of all European states would be affected and would need to be taken into consideration. The deciding question would be how and to what extent it can be possible to accommodate the development of an autonomous West European community into superpower relations, without too severe de-stabilizing effects.

In the following we shall briefly describe some of the importance the question of developing an 'autonomous' EC may have for certain central areas of European policy in the wake of the CSCE. Naturally, these areas will have to be viewed in connection with each other, not in isolation. The matter at hand concerns the establishment of a new structure for European politics as a whole. And in the same way as bloc and alliance politics rest on certain general principles and assumptions connected with administrative/military issues, so will the above-mentioned perspective demand a certain degree of coordination between efforts in the various areas.

Let us start with *SALT.* Here we can immediately see that developing a more independent EC will affect the US strategic position in Europe in a way quite different from, and more fundamental than, what would be the case if the aim were merely to attain certain arms control measures and limitations of strategic weapons based on the political status quo. In this connection, a major issue would be leadership of Western nuclear strategy. As long as US leadership here remains unquestioned, and as long as it is only the French 'force de dissuasion' that is defined as autonomous, the problem is not acute. But should the EC as such take over responsibility in the field of security policy as well, clarification would be vitally necessary. The nuclear strategy of the EC would have to be viewed as a whole: this means that the leadership of the US tactical nuclear forces in West Germany would also have to be involved. To the degree that the EC wishes to play a plausibly independent role in security matters vis-à-vis the East, it will have to make it clear that it has top command of the deployment of both conventional and nuclear weapons stationed on the territory of its member-states. This need not require the establishment of supranational command, but at the very least, quite wide-ranging coordination of military strategy and policy will be needed. And since it is hardly likely that the US will be willing to station its tactical nuclear weapons in Europe without having command over them, the question arises of the withdrawal of all US nuclear weapons from EC territory.

Within the CSCE perspective outlined above there exists an indissoluble connection between SALT and MBFR. Not only US tactical nuclear weapons, but also Soviet medium-range rockets and Soviet tactical nuclear weapons in Eastern Europe would have to be included in negotiations. Both superpowers, faced with such a development, would probably find it expedient to remove their nuclear capacities to the ocean areas outside the European continent. On the basis of developments in arms technology, ocean-based nuclear weapons are considered to provide more reliable deterrent and retaliatory capacity. Naval forces are seen as being more flexible instruments, politically speaking, than land-based forces: they may be kept under exclusive superpower control without violating or limiting the formal sovereignty or autonomy of other states.

MBFR forms a link between the superpower level, EC development, and East-West relations in Central Europe. The growth of an autonomous EC and following up CSCE perspectives requires, in the long run, complete withdrawal of both Soviet and US forces from Central Europe – unless these form part of a *joint* guarantee-arrangement for Europe, that is. Just as with nuclear weapons, here too the question of command will be decisive. As long as it is the superpowers that bear the main responsibility for the military profile on their respective sides of the East-West dividing line, they will also have political command in the major issue in East-West relations: military security. And as long as this situation continues, the EC will not be able to make any pretence of acting autonomously in relation to the Soviet Union or any other Eastern countries.

A slight reduction in the number of US nuclear warheads would not be of much significance for either the military or the political situation in East-West relations. Such reduction could be important, however, if it could be seen as the first step towards full withdrawal from Central Europe of not only the nuclear weapons of both superpowers, but also their military forces as such. It is difficult to see how the MBFR negotiations can result in any kind of increased security unless they contribute to the establishment of a situation *politically* less precarious in the area. Reduction of force levels of both sides – even if 'balanced' – will not automatically lead to increased military security. On the contrary, there is reason to assume that military reductions alone can create political expectations which cannot be realized and which will thus make the situation less stable. It therefore seems necessary that the political aims of MBFR be made clear as soon as possible – whether they should imply continuation of the status quo, or more fundamental changes.

Further expansion of security-political cooperation in Western Europe, centred around an 'autonomous' EC and combined with deliberate follow-up of the foundations laid by the CSCE, may well lead to a new form of regional balance in Europe, replacing bloc politics.

Following up the *CSCE* – which has stood as a common denominator for all aspects of East-West policy in Europe – also requires that the role of the EC be clarified, both politically and institutionally. Just as an EC seen in CSCE perspective is quite different from an EC in a continued bloc-perspective, so is a CSCE system with participation of an 'autonomous' EC something quite different from the case if the EC should remain a NATO subsystem. This difference is well illustrated by the current soundings on possibilities for *EC-COMECON* cooperation. Clarification of the EC's foreign policy and security policy profile should prove decisive for the result of these contacts.

Because following up the all-European perspective is based on the assumption that a more autonomous EC will contribute to a balancing of interests between the superpowers and to creating a new East-West equilibrium in Europe – which would in turn make possible the elimination of present bloc dividing lines –, the concrete regulation of new East-West relations must be directed towards the structure desired, while the regional balance must likewise be kept adjusted in relation to global superpower balance. And since the aim is a regional balance in Europe increasingly based on non-military factors, regulation of relations between the two major economic-political organizations in Europe will be of central importance. It is in this light that we must view the EC proposal of bilateral treaties between the Community and the Eastern countries.

It is vital to realize that the EC and COMECON operate with highly dissimilar integration models. While for EC the goal is a supranational economic-political community, COMECON is built more on the principle of formal state sovereignty, and cooperation is limited to economic aspects. Even though the so-called 'complex programme' of 1971 sets economic integration as the goal, a distinction is made both here and in bilateral agreements (e.g. the accord of 7 October 1975 between the GDR and the USSR) between economic integration and political cooperation. Political integration is not mentioned as a goal at all.

It therefore seems realistic to expect that bilateral agreements between the EC and the smaller Eastern countries would draw the latter more strongly into economic-political cooperation in which the EC forms the dynamic centre. This need not take place at the expense of COMECON cooperation or of relations with the Soviet Union. However, seen as a process, this will obviously affect basic conditions of East-West relations in Europe. By accepting such a perspective, the Soviet Union would have to expect a gradual loosening of bonds with the other Eastern countries. Within the East-West balance this would make up for the EC's 'independence' from the US, and would in fact considerably ease the transition from military bloc politics to cooperation in all Europe. Without an 'autonomous' EC, such a process is inconceivable.

As mentioned, bilateral agreements would mean that Moscow would have to accept the growth of an asymmetrically based East-West cooperation. Somewhat exaggeratedly it could be said that the EC's influence in the Eastern countries will increase in proportion to the growth of such cooperation. COMECON cannot be said to have a similar position vis-à-vis the Western countries. This is why Moscow has made an EC-COMECON framework agreement a precondition. A framework agreement between the two organizations could be used as an instrument for insight and steering in a more general sense. This would probably give Moscow possibilities of holding back if desired. At the same time, formalization of cooperation by means of a framework agreement would function to mark the economic and social system-boundaries between socialist and western-democratic countries.

We now come to the conflict area that more than any other has created difficulties for greater EC autonomy vis-à-vis the US: the *Middle East*. This must be viewed in connection with both general East-West relations in Europe, and the EC's Mediterranean policy. The idea of close and lasting relations between the EC and the

Mediterranean countries – including the Middle East – has played a central role. The EC's declared goal has been to enter as a stabilizing element, through the establishment of close cooperation with both parties to this conflict, if necesary also through formal guarantees of maintaining peace in the area. The agreement already reached with Israel and the on-going dialogue with states of the Arab League are part of this policy, which again should be viewed in connection with EC relations with developing countries in general and with global negotiatins concerning economic and energy cooperation.

The connection between the Middle East and the East-West situation in Europe has found expression in the fact that the Mediterranean area was pointedly included – after strong pressure from the EC member-states – in the field of responsibility of the CSCE, according to the Helsinki Declaration. The geographical framework of the ECSE can thus not be strictly limited to Europe.

It is logically clear that the military-strategic position of the superpowers in the Middle East cannot be looked at in isolation from their position in Central Europe. And this brings in the connection between a political solution to the Middle Eastern conflict and MBFR: without the one, the other is not possible. The superpowers would not be able to undertake military disengangement in the Middle East until a political solution can be found. And as long as they must, for strategic reasons, continue their presence in the Middle East, they cannot undertake any essential de-escalation of their position in Central Europe. At any rate, the latter holds true for the United States:

Both politically and in terms of military strategy, Central Europe and the Middle East must be seen in close connection. Neither of the superpowers will relinquish its position in favour of the other. Just as in Central Europe, an 'autonomous' EC might be able to function as a 'balancer' in the Middle East, helping to make disengagement by the superpowers mutually acceptable.

Of course, if either of the superpowers should see the EC policy line in East-West relations as threatening its own vital interests, it would be in the power of that nation – be it the US or the USSR – to stop the EC. This was partly demonstrated by the US during and after the October crisis in the Middle East in 1973. On the other hand, superpower bilateral relations as a whole are so intimately linked with the regional East-West situation in Europe that drastic unilateral actions in Europe could easily have undesirable consequences in other areas. It is the mutual desire of the superpowers for stability in their relations with each other that the EC must build on in its efforts to achieve greater autonomy.

In this connection the 1973 Middle East crisis is instructive, as it demonstrated that the partial US mobilization of its bases around the globe did not have any great effect on East-West relations in Europe. In Europe, the 1973 crisis was simply not seen as an East-West crisis, and the EC nations took views in part sharply conflicting with that of the US. In fact, US policy here had more the character of putting pressure on West European allies than on the Soviet Union, and in turn the West European countries reacted by not considering the situation as representing an increased threat from the Soviet Union. In other words, detente between the superpowers *and* between East and West in Europe had by now achieved a high level of credibility. In the future, EC freedom of action and room for manoeuvring are likely to increase proportionally with the credibility of detente. At the same time, strengthening the EC on an autonomous basis will increase possibilities for the Community to exert influence on developments in Europe in general.

In the bilateral Washington agreement of 22 June 1973 on prevention of nuclear war, the two superpowers formally prescribed certain norms of behaviour for relations between themselves and with third countries, norms of clear relevance for Europe. This agreement built on certain 'basic principles', agreed on the day before, underlines the joint responsibility of the US and USSR for maintaining peace and security. Of central importance was the statement that 'both sides will be guided by the recognition of each other's equal security interests and by the recognition that efforts to obtain unilateral advantage, directly or indirectly, would be inconsistent with the strengthening of peaceful relations between the United States of America and the Union of Soviet Socialist Republics.'

The superpower norms agreed on here do not set any principle limits as to how far the process of change in Europe may go, but through the demand for balance in advantages and disadvantages a limitation is placed on the behaviour of the superpowers and other states. It is assumed that 'indirect' attempts at unilateral advantages are also proscribed, which means in practice that the total balance must not be disturbed. Thus all actors will have to take this balance between the superpowers into consideration on formulating their own policies. This holds for countries that are members of alliances as well as for neutral states.

On the basis of security considerations and the need for controlable growth and development, the above probably seems to the superpowers to be the minimum conditions for even thinking of the possibility of a new arrangement for security and cooperation in Europe. The CSCE perspective challenges the superpowers to accept a gradual reduction of their chances for unilateral control within their respective spheres of influence, while at the same time making sure that the new system shall not threaten global stability.

IV. Trends, areas of conflict, alternative possibilities

In the preceding pages we have analysed the main trend in West German and Western Ostpolitik, and discussed future implications of this trend for Atlantic and European policy. We chose to discuss this trend precisely because it is linked – as we have repeatedly emphasized – to a comprehensive, long-range conception, one still valid for East-West policy as a whole (cf. many statements of the type 'There is no alternative to the policy of detente') and formulated largely by Bonn.

Up till now we have purposely ignored the question of *probability*: can this conception really be followed up and put into practice? It is to this task that we now turn.

We have already identified some areas as being of especial importance for clarification of this question. Methodologically it appears defensible and expedient to try to ascertain the main trends within these critical areas, then contrast them with the all-European perspective to see whether they conflict or complement each other. This may also help us to clarify any realistic alternative trends.

We shall be dealing with three areas/levels in particular here: the national West German, the European Community, and the Atlantic levels. No in-depth analysis of trends in Eastern policy or in superpower relations will be attempted, as it is felt that the Soviet Union and other Eastern countries exhibit a considerable degree of continuity in following up the all-European perspective.

The three levels will be treated first individually and then in interrelation. During the former, however, it will often be convenient to emphasize circumstances of special relevance to the connections between the other two levels. Since West German policy is the focus of our study, it seems natural to begin with the *national West German level,* continue to the *EC level,* and conclude with a discussion of *the Atlantic level* and relations with the US.

As our historical survey has shown, Bonn's foreign policy and security policy – including policy in the German question – is characterized by what may paradoxically be termed continuity in change: from occupation and one-sided dependence, to sovereign and equal mutual dependence; from cold war activism to a leading role in detente policy; from military and economic weakness to a great power position in both these areas. This process of change has created historical facts that cannot be reversed.

There has also been considerable continuity in the content of Bonn's policy – as shown in the German question, in European integration policy, in NATO policy. All the same, this development has been characterized by an at times almost crisis-like waiving of standpoints no longer tenable within West German policy. Here we may recall: 'policy of strength', the right to sole representation of 'Germany', Atlantic integration, European federation via the Brussels supranational line. Above all there is continuity in the insistence on the 'German option' – i.e. the possibility of working for German unity; support of Atlantic security policy under US leadership; and active support of European integration and close collaboration with France. All these ingredients form part of the abovementioned 'all-European' line – or, if one wishes, Ostpolitik – in an apparently harmonic mix.

However, West German security policy and *Europapolitik* are still not without built-in contradictions. How can national 'inter-German' rapprochement be reconciled with: (1) maintenance of the two disparate social and political systems, (2) continued alliance membership, (3) economic and political union in the EC? How can submission to US NATO leadership be reconciled with (1) cooperation with France concerning the construction and development of an autonomous EC, (2) de-escalation of military blocs in Europe, as assumed in the all-European concept?

Such questions are probably best left for history to answer. True, it might be said that the all-European concept has partly succeeded in reconciling these somewhat contradictory aspects. But its 'package deal' character means that it constantly necessitates new agreements under way – and the outcome of these cannot be known in advance. For instance, what does it mean that the alliances shall be maintained 'as long as necessary'? It is conceivable that MBFR may really lead so far as to total US military withdrawal – which is what is truly politically significant in this connection?

We shall not attempt any definitive answers to these or similar questions. Let us confine ourselves to registering the views and judgements of leading West German elites, as these may be expected to reflect ways of thinking which also occupy the top-level political leadership.

As is well known, there has been considerable disagreement concerning Ostpolitik and its underlying assumptions. All the same, there are few today who count on attempts being made to revise the contractual basis laid down in the Eastern Treaties. The expectations linked with Ostpolitik, however, vary greatly. Two main directions are identifiable: one advocated by spokesmen of the so-called 'progressive' detente policy, the other the more 'conservative' policy line.[21]

The progressive school, whose most prominent representative is Willy Brandt, views detente policy as directed towards fundamental changes in the bipolar security system. The alliances are to be made redundant by a situation where bloc-politics is surpassed. The two systems will gradually, through reciprocal influence and growth otherwise, undergo a re-shaping. Thereby a 'whole' Europe will be able to be created.

Conservative detente politicians have as their goal not fundamental changes, but a modus vivendi, a possibility to achieve pragmatic partial solutions and a reduction of the threat of war.

Just as varying as the motives and expectations are also views concerning the achievements of detente to date. The conservatives feel that developments have simply reinforced their way of thinking. All that has been achieved are minimum solutions, reaffirmation of the status quo, a certain improvement in the climate of East-West relations, and an apparent reduction of the danger of open conflict. On the other hand – still according to the conservative view – the basic elements in the existing security-political system have not proved amenable to change. The CSCE has become an instrument of stabilizing the status quo; MBFR has proved a 'non-starter'. Changing the bloc-system is not possible unless one is willing to risk vital security interests, say the conservatives. 'In fact, progressive detente policy has lost very much of its long-range security-policy perspective'.[22]

The progressives, however, counter with the view that it is too early to draw any such conclusions as to the long-range goals of detente policy. Precisely because detente aims to change fundamental conflict structures in European and global security policy, long-term and careful planning is necessary to avoid creating new insecurity by abrupt measures. This policy, however, will always remain conflict-laden and problematical, both because the opponent in a long-standing international antagonistic relationship is now to be made into a collaboration partner, and because detente changes existing priorities, loyalty relations, and interest constellations in domestic politics as well. 'It is in the very nature of detente policy that it will create new problems as it advances'.[23]

On the basis of current debate in the FRG it is difficult to determine how the balance between opponents and proponents, between conservatives and progressives in the question of detente will develop. The social-liberal coalition can be undermined as a result of stagnation in detente policy. The opponents' argument that Ostpolitik meant selling-out West German national interests may lead to an increased need for both main groupings to seek voter-support in an alternative basis. A new government may take the helm, perhaps with increased instability as the result.

However, there seem to be small chances for major changes in the basic thrust of current policy – whether in the German question or in other issues of foreign policy. There is nothing to indicate that Bonn will abandon the increased freedom of action which the Eastern Treaties and the policy of detente have given West German politics – no matter which government might be in power. During Breshnev's visit to West Germany in the summer of 1978 this was demonstratively reconfirmed when representatives from the opposition – including Strauss – expressly declared themselves interested in continuing the East-West dialogue and cooperation. The 25-year agreement on economic cooperation now concluded between the Federal Republic and the Soviet Union supports this. All in all it is difficult to imagine that the Eastern Treaties could be taken up for revision in the foreseeable future.

There are in the international situation also many other kinds of links and ties of a more permanent nature, influencing Bonn's foreign and security policy, and limiting the possibilities of choice. Relations with France is one such item. From Adenauer's day to the present, the trend has unmistakably been towards increasingly close cooperation. France has vital interests in a continued West German Ostpolitik directed towards detente and the elimination of blocs, and could scarcely be expected to accept a fundamental reorientation from Bonn's side – e.g. in a more 'Atlantic' direction. Nor would any of the other Western European countries look favourably upon any changes in the aims of Ostpolitik and detente policy, even though opinion may be divided as to its more long-range goals of change. It was detente and the all-European line that made West German leadership acceptable to other European states in the first place. Any attempt on the part of Bonn to exert such leadership on another basis would be certain to meet scepticism and direct opposition, especially if it were combined with activation of the German question. This has been recognized by responsible West German politicians and independent observers alike. Even an activation of West German detente policy aimed at peaceful changes in the status quo is currently deemed by Bonn as rather impracticable. Professor Rolf Dahrendorf, who supports the FDP, has stated: 'any policy in the German question which requires of neighbours and allies not only lip-service to the issue of German reunification, but support of the policy of reunification as such, will encounter bitter opposition'.[24]

What possibilities, then, has Bonn of pursuing an active policy in the German question which at the same time is compatible with West German foreign and security policy otherwise? Is not Bonn running the risk of a situation where blocking the German question can tear away the foundations from West Germany's entire *Europapolitik,* creating a crisis not unlike that during the Erhard administration?

An official hearing of the special committee of the Bundestag for inter-German questions, held in late September 1977, took up the German question at length. It yielded interesting information from West German experts on their views of the available alternatives for West German policy, and their evaluations in this connection.[25]

There has been great agreement concerning a 'decoupling' of the German question since 1973, not as the result of intentional policies in West Germany, but as 'a consequence of the change in the constellation of world politics' – here principally the dominant position of the North-South question.[26] From being more or less the centre of world politics for over 20 years, the German question has come to be considered as more or less an issue for the two German states themselves, and that quite apart from East-West problems in general. Other states are satisfied with an inter-German dialogue, on condition that it neither worsens East-West relations too greatly, nor leads to too great a degree of detente, thus endangering the status quo. Here the four-power responsibility represents a potential security mechanism for either eventuality.[27]

While according to reports there seems to be considerable agreement on the international tendency to 'decoupling', opinion is divided when it comes to its more long-range implications for West German politics. Once again, the division between the two schools of thought in detente policy finds expression. Spokesmen for the 'conservative' line argue that hereafter the success or fiasco of detente will no longer be linked to developments in the German question. Even if the present state of recession or stagnation in general East-West detente is followed by a phase of new progress, there would still be no reason to expect any noteworthy degree of positive change in relations between the two German states. And conversely, improvement of inter-German relations would not automatically mean improvement in East-West relations in general. This is so because the Eastern Treaties – including the *Grundlagen-vertrag* – are internationally considered 'partition agreements'.

On the other hand, 'progressive' voices maintain that there has indeed been a kind of international 'decoupling' of the German question, but that this is determined by conditions of a transitionary kind. It must therefore be considered a challenge for West German politics to work actively for keeping up the links that make the German question a component of the larger issues of detente, so that progress in relations between the two German states will at the same time mean progress in general detente, and vice versa.

In this connection it is interesting to note the considerable unrest expressed by SPD members concerning the lack of international understanding as to the motives behind West German policy in the German question and in the Ostpolitik. If it is so – it was maintained – that both East and West can accept only a policy of status quo, viewing with great suspicion Bonn's attempts to keep the German question open, then the issue at hand is more than mere 'decoupling'. The entire foundation of the new policy is at stake, and this can lead to instability. As SPD representative Friedrich (Würzburg) stated:

In my opinion, it is a very serious matter when such questions are raised concerning a country of the Federal Republic's rank and responsibility. Do our neighbours, – – – – – – – – – – see in the definition of the Federal Republic of Germany something of a factor contributing to instability? If so, we and all fractions should ask ourselves: Under such conditions, how can the concept of 'keeping open' (*Offenhalten*) the German question be so defined as not to contribute to European instability?[28]

This fundamental question was not answered directly, but did receive indirect explanation in that there was almost full agreement to keep the German question 'open' in relation to Ostpolitik. More clearly marked were divergencies of opinion when it came to the matter of how contractually-determined policy in the German question could, in the long run, be compatible with an EC policy aimed at political union. Professor Dahrendorf expressed himself most categorically. In his opinion, the EC processes have at present not yet reached the stage where they exclude any conceivable strategy in the area of the German question. The long-range view, however, is quite different:

In principle, a European integration process aimed at political union leaves but one possibility open for Germany: namely, reunification on the Western model.[29]

Elsewhere it appears that Dahrendorf considers 'political union' as very close to full federation. On the other hand, he views the present form of institutionalized political cooperation within the framework of the European Political Cooperation (EPC) as being quite compatible with 'all conceivable motives for policy on the German question'. According to Dahrendorf, there are thus three main alternatives open to the Federal Republic:

1) European Political Union (EPU) in the sense of a federation, with a kind of 'Austrian solution' for the GDR.

2) Policy on the German question as reunification policy by other means: a 'national' policy along the lines advocated by the SPD in the 1950s, and giving priority to reunification or at least

keeping open the possibilities of later close rapprochement between the two German states. This would mean abandoning the integration line.

3) A wait-and-see line, combined with a 'mondialistic' policy aiming at global arrangements and regulation, preferably together with the United States and based on EPC, still leaving the German question open.

Dahrendorf gives implicit priority to the third strategy: a global role for the Federal Republic, in close cooperation with the United States. He believes that such a strategy would yield greater freedom of action for Bonn – among other reasons, because the USA has already declared itself willing to grant the Federal Republic 'more freedom of action than it demands'.[30] A national/state strategy of reunification would jeopardize Western cooperation, besides having no chances of leading to reunification, since it would be opposed by the Soviet Union. Finally, Dahrendorf considers a West European federation 'an unrealistic goal, promoted in words only, while in reality serving as a camouflage for other political aims'.[31]

In the debate on these alternative strategies it was argued by both the SPD and CDU/CSU supporters that Dahrendorf saw matters in a far too static perspective: EPC is meant to be able to develop into an EPU.[32] An 'Austrian solution' for the GDR (a concept which incidentally was met with sharp criticism from various speakers) would not exclude the possibility of later GDR membership in the EC (the EPU).[33] A strategy of 'keeping options open' (*Offenhalten*) for the time being may well be compatible with both possibilities mentioned above, and not only with a 'mondialistic' line. Further, it is possible to conceive of combining EPC with '*Offenhalten*' as a natural preliminary stage to combining EPU with an 'Austrian solution', which in turn might be replaced by EPU membership for both German states as well as possible reunification within the framework of an European Political Union.[34]

Voices were also raised in warning against binding oneself too strongly to doctrines of 'incapacity for change' concerning the two opposing social systems existing in Europe. In that connection mention should also be made of an alternative which the CDU/CSU viewed as undesirable: namely, a 'Communist reunification policy' mobilizing German nationalism as a link in 'Soviet offensive dynamics' and in keeping with 'Moscow's global revolutionary aims'.[35]

All in all, various strong objections were voiced in the debate, warning against being forced into committing the FRG too strongly to one sole possibility. This, it was felt, would represent too much of a restriction on West German freedom of action.[36]

It can be difficult to determine more precisely what is merely apparent disagreement and what are fundamental antagonisms in this discussion of alternative strategies. Dahrendorf definitely has a good point when he says that West German policy has been too much characterized by the attempt to present incompatible items as elements of a unified policy:

> For a long time, German policy has existed on the assumption of 'Russian dolls': German-French friendship fits beautifully into European integration, which in turn fits beautifully into the Atlantic alliance. That this assumption no longer holds, is obvious. This is probably also true of the other 'Russian doll': policy in the German question is by no means in opposition to *Europapolitik* and belongs to a global conception of detente.[36]

With respect to the current situation one may say that both these 'doll'-conceptions of Dahrendorf's are imaginable in two variants; however, each variant encounters problems with the other link: French-West German interaction is indeed compatible with European integration, provided this aims at an autonomous profile for the Community vis-à-vis the outside world. This concept, however, is scarcely compatible in the long run with an Atlantic alliance dominated by the US. On the other hand, a European political union in the form of a West European federation – if the political will were there – could be quite compatible with a re-organized Atlantic alliance (cf. Kennedy's 'Grand Design'), but that would eliminate the French-West German 'doll'. In the other variant, policy on the German question and *Europapolitik* can go together under certain conditions: namely, that of the all-European perspective, but getting this in turn to harmonize with US policy on the global level has proved difficult, especially after the crisis-year 1973.

76

On the other hand, *Europapolitik* and US global policy can well be seen as compatible, provided that the former builds on the status quo and on US leadership. That, however, brings the German question into difficulties. When Dahrendorf concludes that

> Policy in the German question and *Europapolitik* are compatible only under conditions rarely mentioned: namely, either if the former should tend in the direction of an Austrian solution, or if the latter should be directed towards intergovernmental relations,[38]

he is neglecting to clarify some of his more fundamental premises. That is, in both cases he sets the precondition that ties to US leadership will not be questioned, and that with 'intergovernmental relations' nothing more is meant than cooperation of an undemanding, traditional kind. As we have seen, this is not a representative standpoint for Bonn – whether for the governing coalition or for the opposition.

As mentioned in the above, the conception of Ostpolitik that finally led to the Eastern Treaties and the Helsinki Declaration presupposes a multilateral coordination and accommodation of joint strategy: in other words, changes in US politics as well as changes in keeping with the CSCE perspective. Within this perspective of change, French-West German cooperation, European integration, and Atlantic cooperation are defined as compatible entities, as are policy in the German question, European integration, and East-West detente: and this is known to all parties. The conception itself is a logical unity. It is not possible by deduction to determine a priori that the plan cannot be realized: realization depends mainly on how much the parties are willing to support it and follow it up in their practical policies. Should one or more of the important actors attempt but not manage to follow up, this need not mean anything more than that the process will go more slowly than planned – in certain areas at least – while one tries to clear away the difficulties. The situation would be quite difficult should one or more important actors abandon the joint conception and consciously pursue a different line. Then conflicts would almost automatically arise, and the concept of communality would most probably also be abandoned by the others, sooner or later. In such a case, any predictions as to the further development of the concept would necessarily be highly speculative.

Later we shall come back to the question of whether a 'deadlock' situation like this has developed since the US, from 1973 onwards, has no longer actively supported realization of the CSCE perspective. In both variants of the three-part 'Russian doll' concept it is the third link – that of Atlantic/detente policy – that causes problems. For the time being, similar difficulties do not seem apparent in connection with the matter of French-West German relations, nor with official policy on the German question (although ambiguities in the latter may still appear considerable both in the East and in the West). Nor is there anything to indicate that EC policy has officially abandoned or departed from the 'community line' which has formed a major precondition for realization of the all-European conception – i.e. growth and development of the EC into an autonomous entity in international politics. To what degree this concept holds water is a matter to be dealt with below. One thing, however, is easy to determine: that development of the EC will strongly influence the future course of developments in West European-US relations, and thereby also West German-US relations. For that reason, it seems reasonable to discuss both trends and alternative possibilities in the FRG's 'Western policy' on the basis of such a preceding analysis of EC policy. Here attention will naturally be directed towards the possibilities of accommodating policies in the German question, French-West German cooperation, and military security needs into an EC development that can at the same time remain compatible with US interests and demands. If this cannot be considered as a likely possibility, what real chances are there of EC growth continuing in a direction that will in the long run make the community less dependent when it comes to security policy, and thus more capable of following up the all-European idea even without active US support?

The West European integration level

The growth and development of the European Community has been and still is in many ways especially relevant to West German policy vis-à-vis the outside world. This is partly a question of general relevance within the integration perspective, a relevance thus

78

applicable to all members of the community. Why this should be so is most easily understood if one imagines the integration process carried right up to the level of federation, with central authorities responsible for relations with the outside world. And it is partly a question of a more special type of relevance connected with certain peculiarities of the special position of the Federal Republic in international politics. The Western need for an integration framework within which control could be exerted over West German policy has long been recognized – but, as also mentioned earlier, integration was for Bonn the road to equality on the international scene. Further, integration was a vital link in the organization of the bipolar bloc structure. In recent years EC integration has – as mentioned – formed an equally important part of the all-European concept, where the EC is seen as a balancing element in a larger European peace arrangement, expressly linked in with the idea of a lasting solution to the German question.

Given such clear relevance of the EC to West Germany, it is evident that the character and aims of the EC, its growth and development, will be of great importance to the future formulation of West German foreign policy in general, including security policy and matters of foreign economy.

We shall now attempt to clarify how the EC as an integration framework may affect future perspectives for West German foreign policy and security policy. Our approach will follow the lines already laid down. First we identify and establish the current *main trend* in the EC, and project it into the future. Next we shall evaluate the *implications* this trend may have for basic lines in West German policy – i.e. the all-European perspective Finally, possible deviations and alternatives on either level will be contrasted with each other, drawing on the discussion we have already undertaken on the all-European perspective. As we have emphasized, this perspective builds on the assumption that the EC will develop into an increasingly autonomous community with its own profile in international perspective. If analysis of EC development should show that the trend goes in the direction of such autonomy, we may say that on this decisive point there will be conformity between this development and the basic lines of West German policy, and this would very much help to limit our discussion of alternatives.

It is obvious that what we are most interested in is EC development from the viewpoint of foreign policy and security policy. Here, of course, high-level coordination such as that of the European Council and consultations between foreign ministers enter the picture as it has taken shape since 1970. This intergovernmental, or confederal, line was accepted after long dispute within the European Community. It is our hypothesis that this dispute actually resulted in the elimination of certain alternatives that had previously seemed open. This would concern precisely such questions as whether and in which case EC cooperation could include foreign policy and security policy issues. It is this basic approach to the problem that underlies the following highly schematic and abstract categorization:[39]

Form of organization

	Confederal	Federal
Sector	1	2
All-inclusive	3	4

The point of departure here is that the process of integration will lead in the direction of a political community of the confederal or federal type. But there may be different paths to choose among. With respect to Western Europe we may distinguish between four main variants, each connected to the various aims and policies of dominant actors. The terms 'sector' and 'all-inclusive' indicate whether foreign policy and security policy are generally excluded from or included in the concept of integration. 'Confederal'/'federal' concern the distinction between member-governments' leadership and supranational integration.

From the time of its application for EC membership in 1961, Great Britain supported a government-directed policy of integration, with security policy excluded from the competence of the community (box 1 in the diagram). France can ever since the establishment of the European Coal and Steel Union in 1951 clearly be placed in box 3; and just as clearly, the EC Commission and the member-countries supporting it up till 1969 belong in box 2. In the early 1950s there were certain signs of interest in federalism of an all-inclusive nature (box 4) in connection with the plans for a European Army and European Political Union, none of which came to anything. However, there are no theoretical obstacles to imagining a development from sector federalism or all-inclusive confederalism to all-inclusive federalism.

The various integration crises arose when differing strategies of integration could not be reconciled.

The different integration policies sketched above have appeared, with varying degrees of strength, at various times; and are well-suited for use as a foundation to a *phase-division* of EC integration.

Up until 1965/66 the sector-federal 'commission line' was dominant, even in the face of increasing French opposition. The 1965/66 crisis and the so-called 'Luxembourg compromise' resulted in a kind of modus vivendi, which in practice meant avoidance of pressing through majority decisions in questions that some member-states defined as being of vital importance to themselves. In other words, there was an almost explicit acceptance that the national governments should have the final say.

The period 1966/69 was characterized by opposition and uncertainty as to which way to take from now on. Nor were conflicts lessened by the fact that Great Britain – seeking entry – would accept neither the French nor the Commission's line.

1969/73 as a period was introduced by the Hague Meeting, in December 1969, laying down the principle that henceforth no sector was to be considered as irrelevant for the Community, and that there should be created a political superstructure to the existing communities, a superstructure that could accommodate these into a higher political framework. The Davignon Report drew up the guidance lines for political cooperation in accordance with what we have termed 'all-inclusive confederalist' principles. A coordination procedure at governmental level was institutionalized and put into practice. However, it proved impossible to carry out the so-called Werner Plan concerning economic and monetary union, even though the plan itself was voted through. It contained elements of a clearly federal character and would, through its three stages, have helped to lead the Community from confederalism to federalism.

In the period from 1973 to the present the Community, now including 9 members, has confronted major foreign policy problems and international problems accompanying the 1973 oil crisis. Efforts at coordination at the governmental level have been accentuated, as exemplified by the Tindeman's Report of 1976 concerning political union. The EC's confederal character has become ever more visible.

This phase-division of EC development may be supplemented by a partly complementary division concerning the security policy orientation of the Community. Also here we may discern four phases.

1958/66: The 'Atlantic' framework was acepted by all member-states – albeit not equally whole-heartedly by all. The Cold War and bloc politics excluded any discussion of alternative orientations for security policy. The US held undisputed leadership. De Gaulle's resistance to this increased in parallel with EC integration, as he held that EC members in reality relinquished their sovereignty to a communality which was subordinated to US control.

1966/70: De Gaulle's break with NATO integration in the spring of 1966, combined with his all-European efforts in the direction of *détente, entente, coopération* with the Soviet Union and the other Eastern states brought the future of Atlantic cooperation into question. The question of the future of EC cooperation also became acute. De Gaulle's politics were clearly anti-American, supporting dissolution of both NATO and the Warsaw Treaty. His aim was, rather than bloc politics, close cooperation between all European countries, based on the principle of national sovereignty. In de Gaulle's view, the EC should be developed further, but in accordance with the principles of all-inclusive confederalism. A major source of worry to de Gaulle was the development of the Federal Republic of Germany into a dominant European NATO state.

1970/73: The Hague Meeting of 1969 meant not only clarification of the inner organization and development of the community: it also defined the EC as the cornerstone of an all-European system of peace along the lines advocated by West German Chancellor Willy Brandt. (See Chapter III).

West German negotiations with the East were coordinated both inwardly with the EC and outwardly with the US and other NATO partners, running parallel to SALT and MBFR. In accordance with strong Eastern preferences, the entire negotiations/agreement complex was coupled to the organization of the Conference for Security and Cooperation in Europe.

In other words, the period was characterized by the fact that the security policy framework of the EC was extended to include *all Europe*. However, unlike de Gaulle's efforts, this took place on the basis of alliance solidarity in the West and in the East, as symbolized by both the USA and Canada being defined as full participants in CSCE. The USA's leading role both within the alliance and in all-European perspective was not challenged by EC member-states – neither as a community nor individually.

1973/77: After the conclusion of negotiations and agreements between Bonn and the East, as marked by the signing of the *Grundlagenvertrag* between the Federal Republic and the German Democratic Republic; after both states had been accepted as full UN members; and after considerable progress had been made in superpower negotiations concerning arms control and cooperation in various areas – after all this, one might have expected that the nations of the European Community would have been able to concentrate their attention on developing the Community as part of a larger European system, and this in connection with CSCE preparations. And indeed efforts were made in this direction. At the same time, however, the EC was confronted by a series of challenges of *global* significance, challenges that also carried security-political implications above and beyond that of the European framework. Keywords here are Henry Kissinger's 'Atlantic appeal' of April 1973, the war in the Middle East and the oil crisis in the autumn of the same year; further, the establishment of the International Energy Agency, IEA; relations with developing countries; the question of a New International Economic Order and discussion on this in the United Nations, UNCTAD, the Conference for International Economic Cooperation (CIEC) etc; and last but not least, the general economic crisis situation.

In summary, we might say that the EC as of autumn 1973 started moving away from the security-policy framework that it had had in common with the US, i.e. both the Atlantic and the all-European foundations, and started to formulate independently-based standpoints on matters of fundamental importance to security policy – and this partly in direct conflict with the USA, as in the case of the Middle East. However, this is not to be taken as indicating that the EC has 'come of age' as an autonomous entity: there is still too much dependence on the US in the field of security policy for that to hold true. Here there is a clear connection between the regional European East-West level and the global level: only to the degree that East-West detente is plausible and reliable will the EC in the foreseeable future have chances of developing its own profile in vital questions in other areas of international politics. To obtain freedom of action, the EC needs continued European detente. At the same time, it is to be expected that the Community will gradually increase its ability to exert influence on the East-West situation, thus reducing its dependence on the US. We should bear in mind that within the EC there has probably taken place a final clarification as to the question of sector vs. all-inclusive line, in favour of the latter. That means that security and foreign policy will be included in the integration process.

The question of a similar clarification with respect to federal vs. confederal policy has not yet been decided once and for all. At any rate, we can say that the Community today is of the confederal type, and that it will take time for any decisive steps to be taken towards federation. What is involved here is not only the internal growth, but also the accomodation of the EC within the larger international system.

The European union discussed by the Tindemans Report consists in the establishment of a common policy in all the major policy areas of the member-states. A distinction is made between the *coordination phase* (European Political Cooperation), *union* when coordination has resulted in joint policy, and *federation* as a possible third major phase. The Tindemans Report is not a constitution: its aim is politically binding resolutions for all member-states, and in an increasing number of areas. Formally speaking, the Report has never been adopted. It was dealt with by the European Council at their meeting in Luxembourg in April 1976, where the Council assigned the foreign ministers to 'evaluate' the Report – not in the form of a recommendation to the Council, but by preparing for this as many suggestions as possible on the basis of the report, suggestions aimed at clearly defined initiatives chosen on the basis of their importance for the EC and their possibility of success. This was interpreted by many as a near-fiasco for the entire notion of political union. In reality, however, it represents a highly pragmatic scheme of action: not grandiose plans, but precisely calculated small steps as these seem feasible.

Central to this policy of coordination is the idea that outward relations must be developed parallel with inner growth and strengthening of the Community. Developments in recent years may be characterized by the fact that major negotiations concerning the further growth of the Community have been carried on in such international fora as the CSCE, UNCTAD, CIEC, and UN. This reflects not only the importance that the EC has attained in international affairs, but also the recognized necessity of accommodating the Community into the international system.

What the EC member-states have been doing is to make use of the instruments of political coordination which have already been created, in order to fix the major principles and content of policy in one field after the other, in a long-range perspective. This takes place on the understanding that agreement concerning the substance of policy vis-à-vis other countries and other parts of the globe must be clarified before the inner structure can be formalized. The economic and political potential of the European Community is so large that any major changes in internal structure or external behaviour could easily provoke reactions of fear and retaliation from outside countries who felt themselves threatened. For this reason, gradual and pragmatic rapprochement is the most effective strategy. Perhaps the most notable result of this strategy so far is the European Monetary System, which was made operative at the beginning of 1979.

The Tindemans Report makes it quite clear that sooner or later security policy and military policy will also have to be dealt with in a more systematic and formal way than to date. However, it is not considered very realistic to expect this to happen to any major extent in the foreseeable future. Inner disagreement concerning vital questions of security policy excludes that possibility. Considerations concerning security policy will be included in attempts at coordination, but to have the EC assume military NATO functions is still out of the question. It should be recognized, however, that further growth and development of the EC along current lines will gradually help to re-shape the area of security policy in a rather undramatic manner. Possibilities for successful EC security policy depend on the Community as a civilian power, and on the hope of de-escalating the politics of military bloc structure. The lack of actual, physical power capacities and the lack of any formal competence in security policy are both a weakness and a strength for the EC. The Community does not kindle fear among the weaker nations – e.g. in the Third World – in the same way as superpower policy often does. The EC can play on the existence of reciprocal interests on the economic and general political levels. By means of long-term cooperation agreements concluded on a formal basis of equality, it can create mutual interdependence and mutual interests in a way that may prove far more effective than great power diplomacy backed up by military means.

A trait common to all the areas that have been included in the coordination procedure is that the processes under way will in the long run contribute to changing the security-policy environment of the EC. And potentially they also have a bearing on vital superpower security interests around the globe.

Within the development and growth of the EC itself there are also tendencies towards a more direct security policy engagement vis-à-vis the outside world – including military measures. This was illustrated in the spring of 1978, when the French policy of intervention in Africa subsequently received some measure of approval from the EPC conference of foreign ministers.

By getting the other EC member-states to grant a kind of institutionalized acceptance of such military-political initiatives, France appeared to be aiming at giving the Community a new dimension in security policy, or at least creating a 'grey zone' between the actions of individual members and the policy of the Community as a whole. In this case, the background was of course the danger of escalation of superpower confrontation in Africa and in the Mediterranean, with the threats that such escalation would imply for EC policy here as well as for France's own interests.

In the absence of any centralized military leadership, France's actions might be viewed as the prelude to a practice whereby the individual member-states could act, so to speak, on behalf of the community in military affairs – providing that their actions are compatible with the coordinated policy line of the EC. That France should take the lead – and with Africa as the scene – is in keeping with tradition from the days of de Gaulle. Potentially such actions are directed against both the Soviet Union and the US, however. And it should be obvious that taking any such action is out of the question for Bonn.

Otherwise it is reasonable to expect that if this does mark the prelude to a new EC practice, UN Security Council members France and Great Britain would be obvious choices for executors of such military-political measures, at any rate until such time as a special EC procedure be formalized through the European Council. With the exception of the Federal Republic, no other member-state alone has the resources or necessary political weight: the Federal Republic has both, but would hardly wish to risk the quite special political consequences such action would necessarily imply.

Let us now return to the initial questions mentioned in our discussion of the importance of the EC with respect to perspectives in West German policy in the areas of foreign affairs and security. Necessarily only brief answers to some of the questions raised will be attempted.

Generally speaking we may state that the EC has developed into an all-inclusive framework for West German policy – in fact, the most important such framework multilaterally. Both potentially and actually the EPC spans almost the total register of vital areas of activity: the German question, relations with France, the organization of West European policy as a whole, Ostpolitik, the CSCE, relations with the US, relations with developing countries, and with the Arab League, the UN, global regulation of economy, resources – and more besides. The institutional set-up of the Community, its 'confederal' character, and its flexible integovernmental coordination procedures, all this is well adapted to serving the different national interests of the member countries in a period of European transformation. It also serves to increase the FRG's room for manoeuvring by neutralizing some of the impact of West German economic and political dominance. And it makes the position of the FRG less exposed in its relations with the US in a situation where the Ostpolitik raises questions of fundamental changes in the field of security policy. The same holds true in the more global questions of a New International Economic Order. All taken together, the EC makes it possible for the FRG to convert effectively its great potential into political influence.

Extrapolation of the main trends in EC growth and development would have to conclude with the following view: the EC will become an increasingly important and increasingly more autonomous entity both in European and in global politics, with an increasingly high degree of identity between the outward profiles of the Community and of West Germany.

This is quite in keeping with the main official West German conditions laid down in connection with the all-European perspective, and indeed with likely future developments in West German politics, including relations with France. This identity of interests, as should be clear by now, is in fact so obvious as not to require any further proof. Furthermore, more than just the all-European perspective is involved: major lines in a whole series of important areas of international politics are also affected.

Mention should be made of one important reservation: this concerns security policy in the narrow, traditional military-strategic sense, and especially in East-West connection. The EC has not yet developed a *common* line of security policy, which makes it difficult to undertake any extrapolation of trends. This problem is, however, related to the Atlantic level, and will therefore be dealt with further in the following portion of our study. At this juncture we merely wish to stress that in principle the EPC places responsibility for security policy as a whole within the framework of the Community. Among other things, the following circumstances point in this direction:

- principle EC resolutions on the goals of EC development, as made concrete by inter alia the Davignon and Tindemans Reports;
- the character of the organization of EPC: i.e. intergovernmentalism of the all-inclusive confederal type;
- increasingly greater difficulties in distinguishing between aspects of military security policy and other economic/general foreign policy matters;
- the globalization of foreign policy and security policy issues since the 1973 'oil crisis';
- the tradition of French European policy and French-West German cooperation;
- West Germany's need for a framework for security policy in harmony with the national goals of policy in the German question;
- the EC's already to some extent recognized role as uniform actor in connection with the CSCE;
- the general need for strengthening Western Europe as a coun-

terweight to the dominant position of the Soviet Union and the lack of any alternatives to the EC with respect to West European integration;
- increasing disagreement between Western Europe and the US on more and more important issues;
- the decline in the relative power of the US, and weakening of US leadership.

In evaluating whether the current trend in EC development is likely to continue, the above-listed points are clearly relevant: indeed they should carry considerable weight. However, is it not equally likely that the conspicuous national interests, the maintenance of national sovereignty and subordination of Brussels institutions to the – legally, at least – not binding coordination attempts of governments will sooner or later result in dissolution or at least watering-down of the content of the Community? Here Great Britain's tendency towards obstructionist policy in energy, fishery, and monetary questions may serve as reminder of this possibility. Will not expansion of the EC from the Nine to the Twelve increase already severe disparities between the individual economies of member-states to such a degree that a unified economic policy becomes an impossibility? Do not the fiascos of the Werner Plan in 1970 and the so-called 'snake cooperation' in the monetary field prove that it is unrealistic to count on much progress towards economic and monetary union in the foreseeable future? And will not this in turn limit the possibilities of political union? Is there any reason to expect that security policy interests, whether externally or internally, can be made sufficiently compatible to warrant the idea of an EPU with responsibility for military strategy as well?

These and other such questions have, of course, no definite answers. Generally speaking, however, we should be able to say that realization of the indicated aims seems less utopian today than at any other time since the early 1950s. The establishment of the European Monetary System in February 1979 must be regarded as an important step forward. In brief, the major difference from former periods is that since 1970 the continent has seen the formation of an increasingly dominant centre of gravity – both economic and political – headed by West Germany and France. Without the basis of French-West German understanding and cooperation, today's EC could scarcely have existed. This Bonn-Paris axis has a steering function for all EC growth and development. Time and again British attempts to change the EC's course have failed – as shown by, for example, the question of separate British representation at the CIEC. It seems that Britain's ability to influence developments is still on the wane. In the immediate post-war era, Britain wished to 'lead' Western Europe through NATO and the Council of Europe. When the EC was established, the British again wished to accommodate it into 'their' circles, or, alternatively, to have it dissolved. When both these courses proved impossible, the goal became EC membership, so as to be able to influence the Community from within. In the end, Britain had to accept in principle the EC's own conditions for membership. Of the possibilities of influence open to the British, the most important is doubtless that they, working together with the US, may seek to keep the Community safely within the framework of the Atlantic alliance. And this further underlines the importance of developments in the field of security policy – not only for EC-US relations, but also for perspectives in West German politics.

With respect to both Great Britain and the other West European countries, it seems likely that an essential motive will be to maintain the EC as a framework that can help to absorb ever-increasing West German potential. Herein, however, lies a dilemma for the smaller, pro-integration countries. If the EC is to serve as an instrument for shared influence over West German policy, the Community must be granted a more solid foundation and a greater area of competence, which in turn means adhering more to a policy increasingly determined by current internal great-power relations within the Community. On the other hand, by opposing integration and perhaps even advocating dissolution of the Community, one would only achieve a situation where West Germany became an even more dominant actor, the obvious main partner for the US in Western Europe.

There seems in fact to be no real alternatives to the current direction of EC growth and organization. The sector-federalist, supranational 'Brussels line' appears as a permanently discarded stage, as does the British idea of sector-confederalism. Both these lines conflict with the form of intergovernmentalism developed in the 1970s, explicitly all-inclusive in nature. Thus it is reasonable to expect that the EC will in the future be moving along a continuum from all-inclusive confederalism to all-inclusive federalism – a prolongation of the trend described above. Within this framework, 'graduated' membership arrangements along the lines suggested by Brandt seem not improbable: that is, certain temporary arrangements for member-states not yet capable of practising EC resolutions to the full. This, however, would not alter the main features of the problems dealt with here.

If we take into consideration the international status which the EC has achieved, all the agreements and treaties to which the Community is a part, and all the third country interests also involved – then any dissolution of the EC or drastic change appears highly unlikely indeed. Theoretically, of course, the possibility does exist.

Our overall conclusion could then be that an extrapolation of main EC trends harmonizes well with an extrapolation of the main trend in West German politics – with respect to integration policy, West German – French cooperation, and the all-European CSCE perspective. On the EC level there exists, according to our analysis, no realistic or probable alternative to the main trend already sketched out.

In turn this means that the other alternatives discussed on the West German level in connection with policies on the German question have no counterparts on the EC level. Federation for the EC seems quite out of the question for the foreseeable future, so that an 'Austrian solution' – as indicated by Dahrendorf – is not realistic either as an alternative. The growth and development of EPC, combined with gradual inter-German rapprochement on the basis of the *Grandlagenvertrag* and within the framework of multilateral and bilateral agreements between the European Community and COMECON member-states, still appears to be the most realistic course. Any strategy of national reunification or 'mondialistic' policy together with the United States would seem possible only if – contrary to expectations – the growth and development of the EC should stagnate or end in dissolution of the Community. If in fact such a thing should happen, the reasons would probably lie on the Atlantic and/or global level, rather than within Europe itself.

By 'Atlantic level' we refer first and foremost to the security policy framework that the West European countries have had in common with the United States and Canada throughout the entire post-war period. US leadership has been uncontested, and NATO the most important concrete instrument of this policy.

From the very beginning, the Federal Republic based its whole existence on the US security guarantee. Even today, with far greater mutual dependence or interdependence, Bonn still underlines heavily – perhaps more so than any other Western capital – the necessity of a strong US engagement in Europe, both militarily and politically.

In any study of perspectives for West German foreign policy and security policy, it is obvious that these must be viewed in relation to developments on the Atlantic level. It is here that any changes or deviations will have to be cleared; here that conflict-points and possibilities can first be noticed. In the following, we shall continue our discussion of trends and developmental possibilities at this Atlantic level, having already dealt with both the national West German and the regional West European levels. This will necessitate a corresponding shift of the analytical centre of gravity. Extrapolation of trends on the Atlantic level will obviously take as its point of departure *US policy,* since it is the US that has dominated the picture throughout the entire period.

Our first step will be to identify the main features of US alliance policy, emphasizing the intended goals of such policy. Here we shall have to view US policy towards Europe in a global connection, since throughout the post-war period US policy has been a global policy.

Next we turn to the question of whether US and West German policies on the German question and on the EC are in conflict or agreement – i.e. whether main trends in US NATO policy and policy towards Europe seem at all compatible with the trends we have described for the other levels, or whether there exist deep antagonisms that can be resolved only by major changes in the policy of one or both of the parties.

On the basis of such an analysis we can then sketch and discuss alternative developmental possibilities. Since it is West German security policy that is our main focus of attention, we shall attempt a fairly thorough elucidation of how relations with the US may be evaluated on the part of West Germany.

By means of the Atlantic framework, the security policy of West Germany and of the other West European countries is coordinated with US global policy, both as regards East-West relations and with respect to North-South issues. The Atlantic level thus provides a suitable foundation for comprehensive analysis of West German foreign policy and security policy as a whole.

Throughout the post-war era Europe has occupied a special position for the US, both because of the Atlantic alliance as such and because of the East-West division in Europe which has marked the major line of confrontation with the US's main rival in world politics, the Soviet Union. This is still the case. All the same, relations between the US and Western Europe have undergone a fundamental change in recent years. The end of the 1960s and beginning of the 1970s mark the transition to a new phase in Atlantic policy. Instead of the previous definite asymmetry both in military-security policy and in economic matters, the US is today faced with a West European grouping that weighs as heavily in the international economic system as does the US itself, and which is currently in the process of defining its own profile with respect to security policy. Among the major background factors in this change we may mention:

– US preoccupation with the war in Vietnam
– detente policy in Europe
– the EC Hague Summit and its 'new deal' in integration policy
– the weakened US economic position
– Soviet strategic equality
– globalization of international politics, including North-South issues.

When, early in 1969, the US President gave the green light for the 'era of negotiations' in East-West relations, this meant in practice that much of the initiative fell upon Bonn. True enough, Bonn coordinated its Ostpolitik both with Washington and with the other allies. But this could not disguise the fact that in the process which was set in motion by the Eastern Treaties and which received increasing weight and momentum in the early 1970s, the US was partly on the sidelines. In perspectives drawn up by Bonn concerning elimination of blocs and the creation of a new balance in Europe based on an increased role for the EC, one could discern a future withdrawal of the forces of both superpowers from Central Europe.

Whether the US leaders had under-estimated the dynamics of European politics, or had decided to take a calculated risk while waiting for the remaining bones of contention from World War II to be disposed of cannot be known. What is certain is that Kissinger, through his so-called 'Atlantic appeal' of 23 April 1973, began to tighten the reins once more, and that this created considerable disagreement in relations with the major West European allies, France and West Germany. These disagreements were further heightened in connection with the war in the Middle East and the following 'oil crisis', when the EC countries took a stand which, in US eyes, seemed to support the (pro-Soviet) Arab states in their conflict with US-supported Israel.

The main point here is, however, the very character of the leadership that Kissinger sought to re-establish in US relations with its West European allies. On behalf of the US he demanded that EC 'regional interests' be accommodated within the US 'global responsibility', while also making it clear that if the Atlantic security-policy community were to be maintained, the European allies would have to declare themselves willing to coordinate their policies with the US in the areas of economy and general foreign policy. This became even more important now that North-South relations had become a main focus of interest, since coordination between the US and Western Europe on the international economic level would mean coordination of general global policy.

Such 'globalization' is coupled with an increased US emphasis on the problems of 'interdependence' – both generally and in the form of blurring the dividing lines between the national and international levels. The partial mobilization of US foreign-based forces during the October War, the threat of withdrawing US forces from Central Europe if the EC countries would not agree to a joint arrangement vis-à-vis the Arab oil producers, and repeated indications that military actions might be considered in order to safeguard oil supplies: all these examples demonstrate the US line from 1973 onwards. It is characterized by use of the US position of leadership in security policy to fortify or re-establish US control in global economic and general foreign policy issues as well.

Without delving further into the many frictions which this line has resulted in with respect to the West European allies, let us briefly outline the US global concept, indicating the major points of importance for future development of relations:

- NATO is to be strengthened and maintained as the central instrument of coordination in relations with European allies;
- Detente policy in East-West relations is to be pursued on the basis of the status quo in Europe, and brought under more direct US control through SALT and emphasis on 'Basket Three' of the CSCE, accompanied by a certain de-emphasis on CSCE and a harder US line vis-à-vis the Soviet Union in European questions;
- The US supports EC integration only insofar as this may be assumed to contribute to strengthening the Atlantic community;
- The US wants a general economic and foreign policy coordination of 'Western' policy on a 'trilateral' basis (US, Western Europe, Japan) with OECD and IEA as instruments. Based on the principles of free trade and free competition, the economic policies of the Western countries are to be coordinated both inwards and outwards, in a long-range perspective.
- Global fora such as UNCTAD and the UN General Assembly are to act as debate fora, while real negotiations and decisions in North-South issues and other matters of global importance are to be reserved to the regional and more specialized organizations.
- The US reserves for itself the right to freedom of action as a superpower in relations with China and the Soviet Union.
- The US is to emphasize key countries around the world – among these, the FRG – and give priority to developing bilateral relations with them.

These aims would, if realized, bring about fairly fundamental changes in international structures. And it is true that in recent years they have had considerable influence on international politics. On the other hand, these aims involve so many follow-up uncertainties that it is scarcely correct to use them as a base from which to project Atlantic-level trends without first taking into consideration opposing tendencies, conflicts of interest, and attempts at modification within the same Atlantic framework. Francois Duchêne is not far from the truth in saying that the final part of Kissinger's time as US

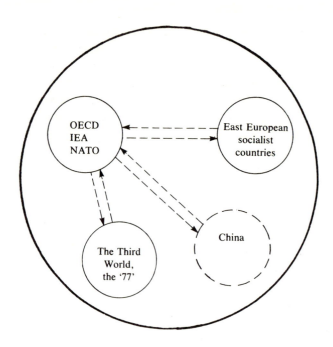

Secretary of State marked 'the beginning of an imperial situation', in which the USA's major partners calmly let their interests be flouted by the 'protecting power'.[40] This would, however, seem to hold more for the short-term than for the long-term perspective.

Western Europe and Japan agreed to intensified coordination of economic policy: but with the OECD as the main instrument – not NATO, as Kissinger had originally intended. This shift was primarily due to European opposition. The European argument was that since economic security policy could not be confined to the alliance – neither in terms of geography nor in terms of subject-matter – any formal inclusion of economic policy into the area of alliance-competence would necessitate re-defining the question of membership, and the function and tasks of the alliance itself. This in turn would be likely to lead to overloading, perhaps even collapse. Additionally, it was pointed out that conflicts of interest between the US and Western Europe already existed on the economic level, and that any extension of NATO to include economy would have to take place at the cost of EC growth and development.[41]

Structurally integrated mechanisms for coordinating military and economic security policy were thus not accepted by Western Europe. What happened was in fact a compromise solution in the form of economic 'summit meetings' between the seven major Western powers (including Japan). These meetings – five have been held in the period 1975–1979 – differ from the European Council in being exclusively an international coordinating forum for high politics. It is important to realize that much of the impetus behind the 7-power meetings was due to French initiative. Interestingly enough, the EC Commission has been granted representation at these summits, although of a limited kind.

Perhaps the most illustrative example of US-West European conflict on organizational matters was connected with the establishment of the International Energy Agency, IEA. The final compromise here reflects two things: on the one hand, asymmetric power relations between the US and Western Europe; on the other, that Western Europe (mainly meaning the EC) cannot accept this asymmetry as something permanent. Two factors may elucidate this.

First, the IEA Treaty contains two resolutions expressly linked with the development of the EC as such. One of these states that the IEA is to be open to accession of the European Community as an entity when the latter has formulated its own energy policy. The second resolution states that the IEA shall not in any way stand in the way of further realization of the EC accords.

Second, France is not a member of the IEA, a fact which gives that country a key position in relations between the EC and US with respect to the IEA, as well as in other issues – somewhat parallel to the situation that arose concerning NATO after de Gaulle withdrew from integration in 1966.

Were the EC to have its own energy policy plus membership in the IEA, French approval would be necessary, which means that France would in fact have a sort of indirect veto vis-à-vis the policies of the other EC countries within the IEA. Should it prove possible to formulate an EC energy policy acceptable to France, the EC as an entity could be represented in the IEA, thereby achieving equilibrium with the US. One major step in that direction was taken when

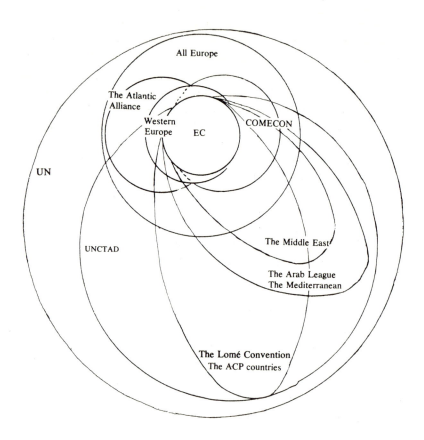

the EC acted with common representation at the Conference on International Economic Coperation in Paris.

For US-EC relations, the establishment of the IEA has thus meant that the US has secured for itself a solid share of influence in the formulation of the energy policies of the EC countries, while the EC has managed to guard itself against the possibility of the US using the IEA to block the development of an autonomous European community. Who will prove to have the greater influence in the long run is a question that will be decided not so much by formal regulations as by real power relations.

As to the North-South question in general, the weakness of the EC vis-à-vis the US has become even more apparent, with many of the same conflicts as mentioned above. On the one hand there is the US demand for a coordinated and unified 'Western' policy under US leadership: on the other, the EC's need to develop a more independent profile. As discussed earlier, the EC countries have been attempting, as a part of their foreign policy coordination, to establish differentiated policies vis-à-vis the various constellations of state-groupings: West European non-EC members, COMECON, the Mediterranean countries, the Arab League, the ACP countries (Lomé), etc. When we consider the implications of a possible monetary-economic union within the EC, it is apparent that the goals of the EC are aimed at a quite fundamental, politically-controlled change in the international economic system, in the direction of greater *dirigisme*. This is at odds with the US determination to build on the GATT and OECD principles of free trade and free competition, undertaking only such adjustments and modifications as practice of these principles may necessitate.

While the EC has functioned fairly effectively in regional and group negotiating rounds, this has not been the case in global fora. Even though the EC is if anything more interested than the US in utilizing global fora as instruments for discussion and decision-making in matters concerning the New International Economic Order (NIEO), actual results after many years of deliberations within the CIEC, UNCTAD, and the UN are close to nil as far as concrete undertakings go. The game of throwing the ball back and forth between the CIEC, UNCTAD, and the UN has shown that when the US is opposed to these fora having any real decision-making authority in vital areas, any and every attempt is doomed to failure. Additionally, it has become clear that under such circumstances the EC has difficulty in acting in concord. A characteristic feature of West German policy is that in matters where previous EC accord has not been achieved, the FRG tends to side with the US.

Since NIEO deliberations have come to practically nothing, it might be tempting to conclude that it is the US policy that will prevail. In other words, the idea would be intensified Western coordination – primarily to set the OECD countries' economy in order – and then on this basis carry on a 'constructive dialogue' with the other two major groupings, the Socialist countries and the Third

World. As to the latter, the goal is to include them gradually in the Western economic system, as they become capable of participating on an equal footing. The weakest will need direct aid and support.

However, attempts at extrapolation of trends on the basis of such reasoning must be highly uncertain. It would mean ignoring the existence of a many-levelled dynamics, a dynamics which seems to be leading development in quite a different direction, and which is likely to make the fiasco in global deliberations more a temporary stagnation than the abandoning of one line (NIEO) in favour of another (OECD). Various circumstances support such an interpretation:

- Global economic problems are becoming greater and greater, and cannot be 'solved' through the regional Western organizations. The pressure for obtaining more universal solutions is likely to increase.
- The US line is viewed by the Third World as being more a negative veto policy than a constructive invitation to cooperation.
- While the relative weight of the US in world politics is decreasing, its economic vulnerability (energy, etc.) is rapidly increasing.
- EC influence in international economy in general, and particularly in relations with the Third World, is rising. A probable result of the Lomé II Agreement recently concluded will be that not only the ACP states, but also other developing countries will view it as a model or at least as a lever for North-South cooperation. The dynamics from negotiations at the global level may very well spill over to the Lomé level, and vice versa.
- As the general integration process within the EC progresses, the need for a marked, independent profile vis-à-vis outsiders – also with respect to the Third World – will increase. This makes it natural to expect that the special and vital interests of EC countries, as expressed in the above- mentioned 'differentiated' global strategy for the community, will be also more sharply marked.
- Finally, mention could be made of the special interests connected with Ostpolitik in a more global view, where the US 'three circles' conception is opposed to both the EC approach and West German policy in the German question. The result of

any common OECD strategy – which has as one of its aims the integration of more and more Third World countries into the Western system – would almost unavoidably be an aggravation of East-West relations. If such a common strategy should succeed, the Soviet Union could reasonably be expected to fear a shifting in the global blance of power, in the West's favour, and consequently tighten its hold on its allies.

Our analysis of the Atlantic level has mainly concentrated on basic disagreement between US and West European (EC) policy, without narrowing in on US-West German relations. As a preliminary summary we could state that an increasing degree of opposition and disagreement is becoming apparent between the US and the EC, in intra-Atlantic, North-South, and East-West matters; and that the EC is likely to gain increasing influence on the formulation of policy in all these areas, if present trends continue. Naturally there exists the theoretical possibility that both East-West and North-South policy may end in deadlock, and that OECD coordination under US leadership and initiative may be driven so far that possibilities of a more independent EC policy either disappear or are severely reduced. However, these scenarios seem highly unlikely in our view. Both sides are aware of the overriding importance of US-EC interdependence, and will in all likelihood be careful not to provoke any direct confrontation. Adjustment will be needed, which probably means continuation of present trends.

If the dominant long-term trend may be assumed to be a relative shifting of strength from the US to the EC, an obvious consequence will be an increasing need for 'a new solidary understanding of roles'[42] on the Atlantic level, not least as to the increasing responsibilities of the EC. If such understanding cannot be achieved, the danger of conflict and resultant weakening of the Atlantic alliance is bound to increase. Any thoughts of turning back the clock to a weakened EC and a strengthened NATO seem unrealistic in the light of the constellation of interests and the relative balance of power. However, the possibility of an uncontrolled West European disintegration as the result of an Atlantic conflict is considerably greater. In such a situation it is conceivable that the US may rely on bilateral negotiations with 'cooperative' states – here primarily the FRG – leaving the others more or less to their own devices. And here a further insecurity factor enters: the possibility that these other states could then be tempted to try rapprochement with the Soviet Union.

The idea of a dominant West German-US axis has a deterrent effect on many – not least on the West Germans themselves. Various prominent West European commentators have emphatically warned about the possibility that the US might try to out-play the EC by relying on bilateral relations with the individual West European countries (cf. Hassner, Nerlich, Ritter, Schwarz, Duchêne, Kaiser, and others). We should note that there is on the US side a strong tendency to emphasize the advantages of bilateralism as an alternative to EC integration. As early as 18 January 1970, in his foreign policy report to Congress, President Nixon presented a programmatic declaration of giving priority to the expansion and deepening of 'bilateral relations with the various states of Europe'.[43]

Secretary of State Kissinger repeatedly showed a clear preference for communicating directly with the individual EC member-states, rather than meeting with representatives of EC organs. Professor Richard N. Cooper wrote in 1972 that the rapid increase in economic interdependence between the Western industrialized nations required common Western solutions, not regional European or global UN solutions: 'The European Economic Community as a center for economic decision-taking is rapidly becoming obsolete in the face of growing economic interdependence; the United Nations, on the other hand, is much too large and reflects much too diverse a range of economic concerns among its members to be useful instrument for international collective action in this area.'[44] Paul M. Johnson makes a major point of reducing priorities on 'multi-purpose' alliances or coalitions, to be accompanied by a corresponding upgrading of 'special relationships' in clearly delimited areas between the US and the main European allies – e.g. as concerns the defence of Central Europe. He argues that comprehensive, multi-purpose alliance relations in today's interdependent world will only expose mutual relations to excessively great strains, and that a system of clearly delimited 'functional' relations is therefore preferable.[45]

On the whole, it seems reasonable to conclude that the sole possibility for combining extrapolated EC-level trends with trends on the Atlantic level into a unified strategy lies in US acceptance of the EC as an increasingly more autonomous and equal partner, within a cooperative framework based on distribution of roles rather than unified policy. This would be in line with both the dominant trend in EC policies as such, and with what might be termed the major trend of argumentation among independent continental European experts in the field of international politics.

Alternative ways of combining these two levels into a realistic conception do not seem to exist in the realm of practical politics. An integrated common policy – an Atlantic union – is out of the picture. Nor is a two-pillar solution of the 'Grand Design' type realistic today. A policy of status quo would be tantamount to fiasco in the question of European integration; nor would it be practically realizable, so long as there are so many processes under way that simply cannot be halted.

The only likely Atlantic alternative to a strategy of 'distribution of roles' would seem to lie in bypassing the EC level in favour of bilateralism between the US and the 'key' West European nations individually, supplemented by Atlantic and European institutions only when necessary for reasons of legitimacy or other multilateral considerations. This line would in fact seem quite in keeping with US policy and argumentation in recent years. It is not necessary to dig very deep to realize that the question of how practicable such bilateralism could be (as an alternative to multilateral role division between the US and the EC) is mainly dependent on the course of relations between Washington and Bonn. Because of the central position of the Federal Republic, a bilateral line would from the very beginning smack strongly of an 'axis policy' built on Washington-Bonn interplay. And here, as we have already shown, Bonn's stand is quite clear: the FRG wishes to carry on an Atlantic policy *through* the EC – not *past* it. The question remains, however, whether the EC is capable of developing further in an independent direction, into a kind of oppositional relationship with the US. Further, it may well be asked whether Bonn's dependency on Washington in matters of security policy may not prove so strong that in the final round the US line will count most. A relevant point here is also the fact that in Great Britain and other West European countries the US has supporting players that it can count upon to 'urge' the Federal Republic in the desired direction. As we showed in our analysis of the internal West German level, there are also elites who consider a 'mondialist' interplay between Bonn and Washington the most advisable course.

The central role of Bonn in relations between Western Europe and the US – and thereby in developments on both the Atlantic and the West European levels – makes it natural to spotlight Bonn-Washington relations in the hope of clarifying positions in what appears to be the decisive question: can West Germany be expected to enter into bilateralism with the US at the cost of EC development and all-European policy?

An analysis of relations between the US and West Germany may take as its point of departure factors at various levels. For instance, one possibility would be to concentrate on the personalities of President Carter and Chancellor Schmidt, explaining much of what has been happening on the basis of their quite different temperaments and work-styles, as well as their personal sympathies and antipathies. Another approach might focus more on concrete, current conflicts of interest: export of West German nuclear reactors, the weak position of the US dollar, human rights issues in connection with East-West relations, etc. While both these levels are important enough, and while both can exhibit points symptomatic in a larger connection as well, it still seems clear that any discussion of future developmental possibilities must build more on structurally determined trends: power- and interest-constellations of a more permanent nature, institutionalized/organized interaction patterns, etc., as well as efforts or tendencies towards more fundamental change in such areas. For that reason we shall pass rather lightly over both the 'personal' and the 'interaction' level, concentrating instead on the main issue just indicated: the chances of West German-US bilateralism at the level of multilateral structures.

Generally speaking, one may say that despite the obvious asymmetry, both the Federal Republic and the US are vitally interested in continuing close cooperation. For Bonn, the main concern is the need of US support in the German question, in Ostpolitik and security policy generally, as well as in European integration policy. For the US, the Federal Republic is an important partner both in the matter of alliance teamwork (including military confrontation with the Soviet Union) and in further OECD cooperation on the economic and ideological levels.

During the most important years of detente – from 1969 to 1973 – interaction was both fruitful and jointly profitable: the Federal Republic wanted to break out of the isolation which the German question had caused, and needed US support for this; the US in turn wished to coordinate alliance policy in a way that could make it possible to find solutions to central problems in relations with Moscow. The possibility here lay precisely in a new deal in Ostpolitik aimed at a settlement in Central Europe. Important for both Bonn and Washington was the aim of drawing France once again into full participation. What this interplay did not achieve, however, was any lasting division of roles. It has gradually become apparent that the conflict potential in US-West German relations is great indeed, and is increasing rather than diminishing. Among the factors that may create conflict the following could be mentioned:

- US difficulties in accommodating EC integration into its own policies. The Federal Republic emphasizes multilateralization of its policies, with the EC as the major framework. The US, however, considers the EC as a potential danger to vital US interests.
- The Federal Republic wants to cooperate as closely as possible with France. The US fears that West German – French cooperation may take place at the expense of Atlantic cooperation.
- Bonn wishes to continue Ostpolitik within an all-European framework as a means of easing the situation in divided Germany. Washington is vigilant against any step that might bring West Germany and the Soviet Union towards a kind of partnership.
- The US wishes to stabilize its relations with the Soviet Union on the strategic level, while the Federal Republic fears that this superpower dialogue may overlook special European – not least national West German – interests.
- The US and West Germany are in fact economic rivals.
- Perhaps most serious: the US has departed from multilaterally coordinated Ostpolitik – among other things, with respect to treatment of the human rights issue – without having presented any new strategy for European policy.
- US assumptions of leadership are increasing at a time when US ability to lead is diminishing, and at the same time as multilateral frameworks – which could serve to legitimize such US leadership – are also being down-graded in priority from the US side.
- The rank and influence in general of the Federal Republic lead

to increasing demands on Bonn for marking out clearly what is to be West German policy. If such demands are ignored too long, the result may well be a loss of credibility.

During his visit to the Federal Republic in July 1978, President Carter strongly emphasized the necessity of further developing US-West German bilateral relations. He spoke of a 'German-American partnership' on the global level, with respect to both economy and security, and stated, 'our mutual interests include all aspects of global importance'.[46] At the same time, however, Carter made it clear that the major security issues – those encompassed by SALT – were to be considered as belonging to 'the wide-ranging responsibility which the United States and the Soviet Union have towards all nations and peoples', and that progress in these negotiations would be decisive for regional European armaments issues and for detente policy as a whole.[47] When he also added that 'no matter how Soviet decisions may turn out, the West will do what is necessary to maintain our security . . . and our own strength' – then the message to Bonn must have been clear enough: We offer you a global partnership, if you in return will leave control in security policy and Ostpolitik with us.

This is not a particularly pleasant message for Bonn. In practice it implies abandoning any continuation of Ostpolitik according to its original conception, without any clear understanding of where US policy will lead. The best to be hoped for would seem a kind of status quo. But for Bonn even a status quo would mean giving up vital goals connected with the German question and with Ostpolitik as a whole. And considering the vacillating US policy towards Europe under the Carter Administration, US security-policy leadership might not necessarily mean a reliable guarantee.

A West German-US axis would probably prove even more conflict-creating in the long run. For the EC, such a line would mean a death blow. New French–WestGerman frictions would seem almost unavoidable. The fear of West German dominance would crop up in other West European countries as well; while at the same time relations with the Soviet Union would be made more difficult, which in turn would affect other parts of Europe too – e.g. the Nordic countries. The fear of a 'Rapallo policy' might also be rekindled. And if the Federal Republic should wish to re-activate its policy of reunification, this could lead to counter-moves in the West, and also in the US, with Western distintegration as a likely consequence. Alternatively, the result might be a new version of a 'policy of strength' – and such a return to a policy of strength on the part of the West today would make the situation in strategically vital areas like Scandinavia and the Middle East far more critical than was the case in the 1950s.

Nor do misgivings in connection with such a perspective decrease when one considers the fact that probably the only way for the US to take the 'lead' in relation to its West German partner would be through demonstration of continued need for strong US military engagement in Europe. This in itself would necessarily be linked with fairly high levels of East-West tension.

On the West German side, however, Schmidt's attitude does not indicate that Bonn is heading in the above-mentioned direction. During Breshnev's visit to Bonn in the spring of 1978, he stated that the Eastern Treaties and the CSCE declaration were to be followed up. It is especially interesting to note his remarks concerning the European Community. The aim is for the EC to become 'a reliable, stable partner for the Soviet Union, within the framework of de-tente'.[48]

Carter and Schmidt have probably indicated the keywords for the two main alternatives in West German – and thereby also West European and Atlantic – perspective. These are either close West German – US interaction within a 'trilateral' framework and under US security-policy leadership; or continuation of all-European de-tente policy with the EC as an increasingly important balancing power-centre with respect to European, Atlantic, and global issues.

The first alternative would obviously be liable to create most conflict on both the national West German and the West European levels, as well as in East-West relations. The entire conflict-resol-ution package so neatly put together in the first half of the 1970s would fall apart. On the other hand, the second alternative would tend to create most conflict on the Atlantic level. Not only European politics, but the entire structure of the international system would be appreciably influenced and affected by the choice between these two alternatives.

The figure below may serve to illustrate, in simplified form, the connections between the various levels treated in this presentation.

ALTERNATIVE DEVELOPMENTAL POSSIBILITIES

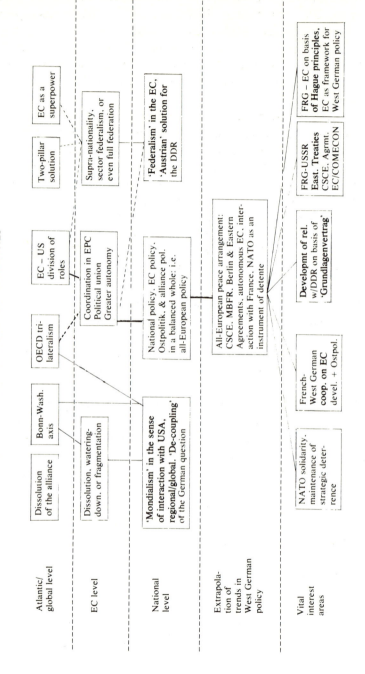

Atlantic/ global level		
EC level		
National level		
Extrapolation of trends in West German policy		
Vital interest areas		

Atlantic/global level: Dissolution of the alliance — Bonn-Wash. axis — OECD trilateralism — EC – US division of roles — Two-pillar solution — EC as a superpower

EC level: Dissolution, watering down, or fragmentation — Coordination in EPC Political union Greater autonomy — Supra-nationality, sector federalism, or even full federation

National level: 'Mondialism' in the sense of interaction with USA, regional/global. 'De-coupling' of the German question — National policy, EC policy, Ostpolitik. & alliance pol. in a balanced whole: i.e. all-European policy — 'Federalism' in the EC, 'Austrian' solution for the DDR

Extrapolation of trends in West German policy: All-European peace arrangement: CSCE, MBFR, Berlin & Eastern Agreements, autonomous EC, interaction with France. NATO as an instrument of detente

Vital interest areas: NATO solidarity, maintenance of strategic deterrence — French-West German coop. on EC devel. + Ostpol. — Developmt of rel. w/DDR on basis of 'Grundlagenvertrag' — FRG-USSR East. Treaties CSCE. Agrmt. EC/COMECON — FRG – EC on basis of Hague principles, EC as framework for West German policy

It will be seen that the extrapolated main trend in West German policy combines all these levels into an apparently logical whole. No real alternative on the national West German level can be said to exist without at the same time presupposing changes on the other levels as well. 'Mondialists' emphasize bilateral interaction with the US, with a corresponding de-emphasis on the EC. 'Federalists' put their trust in full political integration in the EC, thus distancing themselves even further from the dominant trend in US policy than does the current government's line, which is based on European Political Cooperation (EPC). To the extent that the 'federalists' are willing to base themselves on supranational sector federalism, this may give long-range perspectives for a kind of 'two-pillar solution' on the Atlantic level – possibly also for an EC superpower. Here, however, we must add that support for such a line is lower today than ever before, both in West German politics and on the EC level. The 'federalists' thus seem likely to help to increase pressures towards increased coordination efforts within the framework of EPC – rather than to represent any real alternative to EPC as such. In practice, the rift between the 'mondialists' and current German EC policies is greater. Power constellations are such, however, that no West German government would both neglect the EC and jeopardize relations with France at the same time. Should the EC level be reduced in importance, it is difficult to imagine this as anything but the result of events beyond the control of the FRG government. Nor do any of the other EC member-states appear to have as their goal the dissolution or weakening of the EC to any extent.

What then remains is the question of combining West German EC policy on the basis of EPC with Atlantic solutions acceptable to the US as well. More concretely, is it possible to reconcile the US trilateral mutual strategy with the EC role-division strategy? In their basic concepts these two strategies are quite incompatible – but on several points they can, to a certain extent, leave room for compromise. The decisive point will remain the reliability and appeal of EC aspirations for autonomy seen in relation to US demands for leadership.

We have already indicated that the US deviation from the mutual line of detente in European policy has created potential conflicts for West Germany's foreign policy. In chapter V it is to precisely this conflict potential that we turn.

V. Bloc politics or distribution of roles? Concluding remarks

A prolonged period of internal conflict in West German politics was necessary before a new foundation both amenable to international realities and open with respect to acceptable perspectives in the German question could be made possible through the formulation of Brandt's EC policies and his Ostpolitik. There were long-drawn-out and intricate rounds of negotiations, couplings and de-couplings, package solutions, multilateral proposals, and finally, Constitution Court scrutiny of the Eastern Treaties to test the compatibility of the treaties – including the *Grundlagenvertrag* – with the view of the German question set out by the Constitution itself. All this was in the end to give to the new *Europapolitik* almost constitutional status.

This European policy scheme is currently in danger of losing credibility. In the area of Ostpolitik, Bonn has seen how Washington can, without prior consultation, emphasize the human rights issue in such a way that the balanced unified solution – to which it had been hoped the CSCE could contribute – no longer seems within reach. For the same reason, Bonn has lost much of the initiative in Ostpolitik, and now stands without any real alternative in the German question. It is against this background that we should understand current talk of temporary 'decoupling'.

Such blocking of Ostpolitik has taken place despite the fact that the Soviet Union, the GDR, and other East European countries have continued to show considerable interest in carrying on and intensifying CSCE policy on a multilateral basis. Here an increasing conflict of interests between the US and the Federal Republic becomes apparent. Partly as a result of changes in US policy, the possibilities which the CSCE seemed to open up for West German Ostpolitik now appear to be in danger of being forfeited. In the wake of the 'oil crisis', the US has down-graded the priority it has given to 'European' Ostpolitik in favour of a *global* Western policy of consolidation and coordination.

Parallel with this change in US policy vis-à-vis the CSCE there has, however, also been an up-grading of the role of West Germany as a partner of the US in global politics. Both in military East-West and in economic North-South issues the tendency is towards a Washington/Bonn axis. This is the US offer to Bonn: a kind of alternative to both CSCE policy – which Washington fears might serve Soviet better than Western interests – and to a more autonomous EC – which conflicts with the US global conception.

The position of West Germany as the dominant West European state makes the country a 'natural' main partner for the US. However, a US policy that has as its goal military and political consolidation of the status quo will necessarily conflict with vital West German national interests, because these are intimately linked with overcoming the status quo. Development of a US-West German axis is most likely to destroy the very foundations of West German *Europapolitik,* and thereby have negative consequences for both West European and Atlantic cooperation.

To begin with, a system of bloc politics based on a Bonn/Washington axis – with priority being given to the military aspects of East-West relations – will of necessity be at the expense of detente in general. The goodwill that Bonn has accumulated as the leading detente actor in Europe will be in jeopardy. East-West tensions in Europe will again have Germany as a focal point: and this in turn cannot fail to be a burden on West German foreign policy in general, and not least vis-à-vis the East.

Second, the possibility of rapprochement between the two German states will be reduced parallel with general East-West stagnation.

Third, any US-West German bilateralism is sure to have a disruptive effect on cooperation in Western Europe. It will help to reactivate fears of a new German hegemony. Not least, relations between Bonn and Paris will become more difficult. Years ago, Adenauer warned strongly against any such development. In recent years, Bonn and Paris have increasingly come to form the very nucleus of EC cooperations, thereby also creating the necessary conditions for political coordination processes within the Community. West German – US partnership would be sure to tear away the foundations of French – West German cooperation, which would in turn have severe repercussions on EPC in general. The precondition for French support to Bonn must be continuation of detente vis-à-vis the East, together with West German support of EPC.

Fourth, a Bonn/Washington axis would also be a link in US global policy. This already includes North-South relations, maintenance of the existing organizational basis of the Western 'liberal' international system under US leadership, alliances, ideological boundaries, etc. On these and various other issues, US and West German interests are potentially at odds. As already mentioned, West Germany is highly dependent on the US in security policy matters and does not wish risking a break or serious conflicts in this area. At the same time, however, Bonn is aware that counting too heavily on US – West German bilateralism may make it more difficult for the FRG to realize its long-range security policy goals. These goals are connected with the German question, with the growth and development of the EC, and with East-West cooperation within a larger European framework.

From the West German point of view, consolidation and further expansion of the EC seem to be an almost absolute condition for any coordinated West German - US *Europapolitik* – even if this should imply a greater degree of West European autonomy vis-à-vis the US. Such a development of the EC is seen as the most realistic possibility for creating a framework capable of absorbing any West German increase in power, thus helping to keep stability in European politics on an even keel. Moreover, a politically strong and coordinated Western Europe may be said to represent a better guarantee for US interests than would a strong West Germany in conflict with its neighbours. Nor can one ignore the possibility that a West Germany that lacked a secure West European framework might be tempted to look for solutions vis-à-vis the East by itself.

In some cases it may appear that the US, lacking other means of influence, has played its security-policy trump card in order to have its way with West Germany and other West European countries. During the energy conference held in Washington, for instance, the US side explicitly threatened withdrawal of US forces from Central Europe if the West European countries did not agree to the US proposal concerning the clash with OPEC. The SALT dialogue with the Soviet Union, the giving of priority to the military dimension in alliance cooperation, the introduction of new and advanced nuclear weapons-systems in NATO, etc.: all these are sides of the trans-Atlantic relationship that help to strengthen US demands for centralized command.

One thing that makes these features of the picture seem a bit discouraging from the West European – not least the West German – viewpoint, is that the US demand for control is put forward against the background of increasing uncertainty as to what the intents of the US government really are. Symbolic examples are the debates concerning the neutron bomb, cruise missiles, civilian application of nuclear energy, human rights issues, etc.

In the light of Bonn's highly formalistic and cautious attitude in all issues touching on the very foundation of the FRG's existence, including the Eastern Treaties and the legally based standpoints on multilateralization of the German question, it is no wonder that any and every insecurity in relation to US European policy has a negative effect on relations with Bonn. If West German is led away – without being consulted – from the multilaterally accepted 'European' framework and over to a harder bloc-line, determined by US global considerations and interests, the consequence will almost unavoidably be increased conflict both on the Atlantic level and in East-West relations. For Bonn it is not merely a question of maintaining the status quo or not, as might have been the case in former years. Today the question is whether it is necessary to abandon the contractually agreed foundation for detente, a basis which at any rate had opened certain possibilities of overcoming the sharp East-West division of Germany – and this mainly due to Western disagreements. With the armaments spiral continuing, and with increasing asymmetries on the European level – both as concerns the positions of the superpowers and also between the Soviet Union's military potential, on the one hand, and that of the West European countries, on the other – the chances of achieving an alternative or better basis for Ostpolitik seem minimal indeed.

Earlier it might have been possible to predict that in West German politics, anything conflicting with considerations of Atlantic security policy would have to give way. Today, however, the situation is not so clear. Precisely because Bonn has always had to build its policy on multilateral, integrated solutions, there is today a strong scepticism of anything that would involve abandoning a common, contractually based foundation. The various treaties and agreements concerning the German question are highly complex, both politically and in terms of international law. Indeed, what amounted to a political upheaval in West Germany was needed, together with many years of intense negotiations, before it was possible to divert Bonn's German policy over from a one-sidedly Western-based contractual framework and into the common East-West framework created by the Eastern Treaties and the CSCE. And even today, this framework is seen by Bonn as representing but the prelude to a long-range process of rapprochement. To abandon this new basis now, without even any alternative in sight, would most likely mean yet another major upheaval in West German politics. Such a scenario seems highly improbable, especially since Bonn would scarcely consider this to be in the West German national interest.

We would thus predict the following: as long as the East shows interest in continued growth and development of East-West relations in a way that, in Bonn's view, helps both to strengthen security in Europe generally and to make easier the situation of persons living in the GDR and other East European countries – so long will the West German government be likely to continue its detente policy along the lines laid down by the Eastern Treaties. This seems a reasonable prediction, even if this policy should presuppose a greater degree of autonomy and even some conflict in Bonn's relations with Washington.

Naturally enough, a whole series of incalculable factors is involved with respect to developments on both the national West German and the international levels. Crises may arise, whether in matters of policy, economy, supplies, etc. Dramatic technological advances may come to alter the strategic situations. These are but a few examples. However, if we ignore such unpredictable factors, it does seem reasonable to expect the Federal Republic of Germany to occupy an increasingly dominant position in European politics; further, that Bonn itself will attempt to channel this potentially unsettling dominance through the EC and – together with its partners – strengthen the role of the EC within the larger cooperative frameworks concerning East-West and North-South issues, in a way that will exclude any West German 'Alleingang'.

If such multilateral frameworks prove insufficient, this will increase the possibility of conflict. It would thus seem to be in the obvious interest of the other European countries as well as the US to contribute as best they can to strengthening these multilateral frameworks in correspondence with the detente perspectives set out by the Eastern Treaties and by the declarations of the CSCE. They would stand everything to gain by such a move.

Notes and references

1 For a general treatment of the concept of interpenetration, see James N. Rosenau, *The Scientific Study of Foreign Policy,* Chapter V, esp. pp. 127 f. As to the interpenetration of the FRG system, Gerda Zellentin has given an interesting analysis in 'Zielvorstellungen der europäischen Verflechtung in der Bundesrepublik – Möglichkeiten und Grenzen westdeutscher Europa-Politik' in *Regionale Verflechtung der Bundesrepublik Deutschland,* cp. p. 279, where the cited description is to be found.

2 Cf. E. Deuerlein, *Deutschland wie es Chruschtschow will,* Bonn 1961, p. 23.

3 Ibid., p. 51.

4 De Gaulle at a press conference on 25 March 1959, reproduced in E. Jouve, *Le General de Gaulle et la Construction de l'Europe,* Paris 1967, Vol. II, p. 222.

5 Theo Sommer in *Die Zeit,* 18 November 1966.

6 *Die Welt,* 4 September 1968.

7 *Bulletin d. Bundesregierung,* no. 33, 18 March 1969.

8 *Bull. d. Bundesreg.,* no. 53, 17 April 1970.

9 *Bull. d. Bundesreg.,* no. 2, 7 January 1970.

10 Brandt in the Bundestag, 14 January 1970; cf. *Bull. d. Bundesreg.,* 6, 15 January 1970.

11 *Bull. d. Bundesreg.,* no. 49, 22 April 1969, p. 413.

12 *Bull. d. Bundesreg.,* no. 5, 14 January 1970.

13 Speech in the National Press Club in Washington, DC, on 10 April 1970; cf. *Bull. d. Bundesreg.,* no. 49, 10 April 1970 (translated from German).

14 *Bull. d. Bundesreg.,* no. 5, 14 January 1970.

15 Speech in the Council of Foreign Relations, New York, on 8 Aril 1970; cf. *Bull. d. Bundesreg.,* no. 49, 11 April 1970 (translated from German).

16 Cf. *Der Grundlagenvertrag vor dem Bundesverfassungsgericht,* Bonn 1975, p. 397.

17 Ibid., p. 96.

18 Ibid., p. 395.

19 Ibid., pp. 395 ff.

20 *Zur Sache* (Ausschuss für innerdeutsche Beziehungen), no. 4, 1977, p. 71.

21 Cf. Hans-Peter Schwarz in Kaiser & Schwarz (eds.), *Amerika und Westeuropa,* Stuttgart 1977, p. 168.

22 Ibid., p. 168.

23 K. Kaiser u. M. Kreis (eds.), *Sicherheitspolitik vor neuen Aufgaben,* Frankfurt a. M. 1977, p. 420.

24 *Zur Sache,* no. 4, 1977, pp. 20 ff.

25 Reported in *Zur Sache*, no. 4, 1977.

26 Professor Ralf Dahrendorf in one of his replies during the above-mentioned debate, reproduced in *Zur Sache*, nr. 4/77 p. 69; cf. his written contribution on pp. 21 ff.

27 Professor Hans-Petter Schwarz, ibid., p. 44.

28 Ibid.

29 Ibid., p. 35; cf. also p. 65.

30 Ibid., p. 20.

31 Ibid., p. 18.

32 Cf. Keutzmann (SPD), ibid., p. 55.

33 See e.g. Graf Huyn (CDU/CSU), ibid., p. 61.

34 Cf. Schmude (SPD), ibid., p. 56.

35 Cf. Graf Huyn and Böhm, pp. 62 and 54, respectively.

36 Kreutzmann, ibid., p. 55.

37 Ibid., p. 18.

38 Ibid., p. 18.

39 The following schematization builds on the author's line of reasoning in *Europa – politisch. Alternativen, Modelle und Motive der Integrationspolitik*, Berlin 1977.

40 Kaiser & Schwarz (eds.), *Amerika und Westeuropa*, p. 279.

41 Cf. K. Kaiser u. M. Kreis (eds.), *Sicherheitspolitik vor neuen Aufgaben*, pp. 426 ff.

42 Klaus Ritter, in Kaiser & Schwarz (eds.), *Amerika und Westeuropa*, p. 216.

43 *US Foreign Policy for the 1970s. A New Strategy for Peace*, Washington DC (January), 1970, p. 32.

44 *World Politics*, 24 (1972), no. 2, p. 180.

45 Paul M. Johnson, '«Special Relationships» in a Transnational World: Regime Persistence and Regime Change in Washington-Bonn Relations', paper presented at the International Studies Association conference held in Washington DC, February 1978.

46 *Bull. d. Bundesreg.*, no. 81, 20 July 1978, p. 774.

47 Ibid., p. 776.

48 *Bull. d. Bundesreg.*, no. 47, 12 May 1978.

Select Bibliography

Andrén, Nils: Internationell utveckling och svensk försvarsdoktrin, Folk och Försvar, Stockholm, 1978. (International Development and Swedish Defence Doctrine. In Swedish.)

Arndt, Claus: Die Verträge von Moskau und Warschau. Politische, verfassungsrechtliche und völkerrechtliche Aspekte, Verlag Neue Gesellschaft GMBH, Bonn-Bad Godesberg, 1973.

Aussenpolitische Perspektiven des westdeutschen Staates, Band 1: Das Ende des Provisoriums. Band 2: Das Vordringen neuer Kräfte. Band 3: Der Zwang zur Partnerschaft, in the series Schriften des Forschungsinstituts der Deutschen Gesellschaft für Auswärtige Politik e.V., R. Oldenbourg Verlag, München/Wien 1971/72.

Brandt, Willy: Friedenspolitik in Europa. Frankfurt a.m. 1968.

Der Grundlagenvertrag vor dem Verfassungsgericht. Dokumentation zum Urteil vom 31. Juli 1973. Published by Presse- und Informationsamt der Bundesregierung, Bonn 1975.

Die Internationale Politik 1970-1972, Jahrbücher der Deutschen Gesellschaft für Auswärtige Politik e.V., München/Wien 1978.

Deutschlandpolitik. Öffentliche Anhörungen des Ausschusses für innerdeutsche Beziehungen, Bonn, in *Zur Sache* no. 4/1977.

Kaiser, Karl: German Foreign Policy in Transition, Oxford Paperbacks, London 1968.

Kaiser, Karl und Kreis, Markus (eds.): Sicherheitpolitik vor neuen Aufgaben, – Schriften d. Forschungsinstituts d. DGAP, Metzner Verlag, Frankfurt a.M. 1977.

Kaiser, Karl und Schwarz, Hans-Peter (eds.): Amerika und Westeuropa, Gegenwarts- und Zukunftsprobleme, Schriften d. Forschungsinstituts der DGAP, Belser Verlag, Stuttgart/Zürich 1977. English edition 1978: America and Western Europe. Problems and Prospects, Lexington Books.

Lindemann, Beate: EG-Staaten und Vereinte Nationen, Schriften d. Forschungsinstituts d. DGAP, R. Oldenbourg Verlag, München/Wien 1978.

Regionale Verflechtung der Bundesrepublik Deutschland, Schriften des Forschungsinstituts d. DGAP, Bonn, R. Oldenbourg Verlag, München/Wien 1973.

Rosenau, James N.: The Scientific Study of Foreign Policy, The Free Press, New York/London 1971.

Sæter, Martin: Det politiske Europa. Europeisk integrasjon: teori, idé og praksis, Universitetsforlaget, Oslo 1971. (Political Europe. European Integration: theory, idea, practice. In Norwegian.)

Sæter, Martin: Europa - politish. Alternativen, Modelle und Motive der Intergrationspolitik, Berlin Verlag 1977.

Schulz, Eberhard: Moskau und die europäische Integration, Schriften d. Forschungsinstituts d. DGAP, R. Oldenbourg Verlag, München/Wien 1975.

Schulz, Eberhard (ed.): Die Ostbeziehungen der Europäischen Gemeinschaft, Schiften d. Forschungsinstituts der DGAP, R. Oldenbourg Verlag, München/Wien 1977.

Sjøstedt, Gunnar: The external role of the European Community, Saxon House/Utrikespolitiska Institutet, Stockholm 1977.

Tilford, Roger (ed.): The Ostpolitik and Political Change in Germany, Saxon House/ Lexington Books, 1975.

Twitchett, Kenneth J. (ed.): Europe and the World. The External Relations of the Common Market, Europa Publication, London 1976.

Volle, Herman und Wagner, Wolfgang (eds.): KSZE, Konferenz über Sicherheit und Zusammenarbeit in Europa, Beiträge und Dokumente aus dem Europa-Archiv, Verlag für Internationale Politik GMBH, Bonn 1976.